John Ciardullo Associates
Architecture and Society

Copyright © 2004. By Edizioni Press, Inc. All rights reserved. No part of this book may be reproduced in any form without written permission of the copyrightowners. All images in this book have been reproduced with the consent of the artists concerned and no responsibility is accepted by producer, publisher, or printer for any infringement of copyright or otherwise, arising from the contents of this publication. Every effort has been made to ensure that credits comply with information supplied.

First published in the United States of America by:
Edizioni Press, Inc.
469 West 21st Street
New York, New York 10011
www.edizionipress.com

Design and Composition:
Sidney Blank
Bethany Koby

Editor:
Aaron Seward

Editorial Assistants:
Sarah Palmer
Jamie Schwartz

ISBN: 1-931536-13-9
Library of Congress Catalogue Card Number: 2002101185

Printed in China

John Ciardullo Associates
Architecture and Society

By Maggie Kinser Hohle

Introduction

Community Centers

Public Schools

Multi-family Housing

Planned Communities

Private Homes

Corporate Interiors

Acknowledgements\Credits

006 - 021	Introduction by Maggie Kinser Hohle
024 - 031	Boylan Street Pool / Newark, New Jersey (1975)
032 - 039	St. Peter's Park and Recreation Center / Newark, New Jersey (1976)
040 - 047	South Paterson Public Library / Paterson, New Jersey (1978)
048 - 055	Owen Dolen Golden Age Center / Bronx, New York (1982)
056 - 063	Isabelle Miller Community Center / Camden, New Jersey (1982)
064 - 071	Hamilton Fish Park and Recreation Center / New York, New York (1992)
072 - 079	Gerritsen Beach Branch Library / Brooklyn, New York (1997)
082 - 089	I.S. 254 / Bronx, New York (1999)
090 - 097	P.S. 242 / Queens, New York (2001)
098 - 101	Edgemont Junior-Senior High School / Scarsdale, New York (2002)
102 - 105	Seely Place Elementary School / Scarsdale, New York (2002)
106 - 111	Greenville Elementary School / Scarsdale, New York (2002)
112 - 115	P.S. 268 / Queens, New York (2002)
116 - 121	P.S. 166 / Queens, New York (2002)
124 - 131	Plaza Borinquen / Bronx, New York (1975)
132 - 139	Maria Lopez Plaza / Bronx, New York (1982)
140 - 147	200 East 87th Street / New York, New York (1992)
150 - 157	Port Regalle / Staten Island, New York (1988)
158 - 161	Rock Shelter Road / Waccabuc, New York (1998)
164 - 173	Ciardullo House / Pleasantville, New York (1971)
174 - 181	Perless House / Greenwich, Connecticut (1982)
182 - 189	Browne House / Waccabuc, New York (1990)
190 - 195	Torres House / Waccabuc, New York (1993)
196 - 203	Samberg House / Chappaqua, New York (2001)
206 - 209	Dawson Giammalva Capital Management, Inc. / Southport, Connecticut (1997)
210 - 215	Pequot Capital Management, Inc. / Westport, Connecticut (1999)
216 - 223	Pequot Capital Management, Inc. / New York, New York (2000)
224 - 225	Acknowledgements
226 - 229	Credits

006 Introduction

"Architecture is a humanistic art. It's the most social of all the arts. First and foremost, we create an environment for people to live in. Aesthetics is just aesthetics, but how you arrive at a solution to the social issue–that's the work I've been doing all these years."

John Ciardullo

For 30 years, John Ciardullo Associates P.C. has given architectural form to community, privacy, and all the realms in between. Ciardullo began his career in the 1960s, working from a radical viewpoint and within that period's most troublesome area of architecture: multi-family urban housing. He has continued to challenge social and architectural conventions in the city and beyond. The majority of the projects presented in this monograph are urban structures and, as Ciardullo puts it, "not the glory jobs." They are community centers, public libraries, public schools, and multi-family housing. On the whole, the sites have been tight, the budgets small, the programs, or assignments, neither emotional nor primarily aesthetic. The remainder of John Ciardullo Associates' work comprises planned communities, private homes, and corporate interiors. Despite greater financial flexibility, he designs these with the same social parameters.

John Ciardullo Associates' purpose is to reinforce our tendency toward fellowship, and its opposite, solitude. Just as we need to be part of a group, to associate with family and mingle with neighbors, we also need to retreat. It is the architect's job to give us places that accommodate all of these activities. Without crusading in the vocabulary of the social worker, Ciardullo gives the same consideration to those who live in publicly funded inner city housing developments as he gives to clients for private homes. It is not more funding that is necessary–at either end of the real estate market–to architecturally satisfy our need for both privacy and community, but more consideration of our needs and more logical ways of meeting them.

Each type of building introduced here explores a different aspect of these needs. If we live in multi-family housing in the middle of the city, we need a strong sense of our own private space. We need private space for our family, both indoors and out, reached through an entrance we can call our own; and beyond that, we need a space we can share with neighboring families. A small courtyard will do. It is only when we are secure in these spaces that we can comfortably face the public space of the city streets. If we want our children to feel safe and carefree, even in an urban school, the school should be located on a side street rather than an avenue, facing friendlier neighborhood streets. If we need to feel that we are part of a community, even as we read in solitude, we can open our libraries to daylight and the environment around them. If vandalism scares us and threatens to bring on more, we can admit everyone in the community into our common buildings by extending their hours of operation and using them for more than one purpose. If we crave the company of our neighbors, we can have it, in a space we all share. There is room.

John Ciardullo Associates' work is often published in the context of its social implications and effects. It includes broadly programmed community facilities that were innovative at the time they were built and are now popular models; libraries that center their communities; public schools that allow after-hours access for the community; low-rise multi-family housing that turns "projects" into "homes"; planned communities that feel like indigenous neighborhoods; private homes that seem to have arisen from the mature forests surrounding them; and corporate offices that unite their employees in both work and play.

John Ciardullo is a sociologist, as he claims all architects must be. Genuine architecture is born of social truths, and its end result should be a positive effect on society.

The burden of establishing a productive relationship between society and architecture is the architect's; he must reflect social changes with architectural changes. This revelation came to John Ciardullo when he was a second-year graduate student in Harvard's architecture program. At the time he was also teaching structural engineering, a field he had already worked in for two years. His architecture class received an assignment for a housing project in South Boston. While other students were talking about proportions and looking at the forms from above, Ciardullo examined the project's social context.

Every designer approaches his work from two points: learned technique and personal experience. John Ciardullo's personal experience of architecture and community began with a childhood spent living in a small, one-bedroom apartment in the Bronx, New York. He had no private space. On the other hand, his street was lined with apartment buildings, and his relatives lived up and down that street. Ciardullo recognized that there were many levels of public space. In "Urban Housing," a pamphlet Ciardullo published with associates at the University of Illinois in 1967, he defined six environments, arranged in a hierarchy along a continuum, in which one extreme is privacy and the other is community. These realms are private/individual, private/family, private/group, group, public/group, and public/urban.

Seeing his surroundings in terms of this continuum, Ciardullo found a naturally determined scale. He also found that the continuum is in evidence everywhere: in our living areas, in our offices, in our public buildings, and in the encompassing physical environment. Ciardullo does his most compelling work in his original environment: the urban neighborhood. The historical transformation of this environment is the historical context of his work.

Built at the turn of the century, New York City's neighborhoods were organized according to our natural limitations: How far can we see? How far can we walk? How many people can we recognize? How many can we know? When most people traveled around the city on foot and by public transportation, they were very familiar with their immediate neighbors. They knew the local merchants. In their own territory, residents felt comfortable and in control. As they roamed farther from home, the dwindling number of familiar faces and sights fostered excitement, even trepidation, at the possibility of associating with strangers in the public/urban realm.

In the beginning, architects in New York City built as if they understood and treasured these natural limitations. The five-story tenements had only two families on each floor, creating a nice, small group of immediate neighbors. The average residential block was home to only 600 families, even when 22-family apartment houses became the norm. Socially, neighborhoods developed according to common ethnic and religious backgrounds. A church among the residences comforted the members of the community within what Ciardullo defines as the private/group realm–a private place for the use of a particular group.

The grammar schools, where children first experience a formalized community, were built small. Younger school children walked to school and back, secure in a large extended-family atmosphere. Junior high schools and high schools served larger aggregates of communities, but graduation from one to the next assumed the continuation of friendships and associations, and normally family members were in attendance to some degree.

New York's traditional urban neighborhoods began to dissolve socially in the 1950s, when the first generation of immigrants' grandchildren graduated from high school, went to college and university, often married outside of their ethnic groups, and didn't come back to the neighborhoods to settle as adults. The middle class became mobile, liberated from the constraints of public transportation and their own physical fitness. With a car, you could distance yourself a good 50 miles from your home turf in an hour, and those who traveled through your neighborhood, voyeurs on wheels, would go unrecognized, and, as the sight became common, virtually unseen.

Architectural changes followed suit. In the past, the construction of one or two tenements, built to the small physical and social scale, only added ten families to the 600 in the immediate neighborhood. The techniques and concepts of early modernism, however, introduced a scale that was finally possible to build, but impossible to inhabit. Urban renewal was the name given to the destruction of entire blocks to make way for the skyward reaching towers of a new world. Modernism defined utopia as a place where people could live as if they were machines, efficiently stacked one on top of another, 20 stories into the sky. Care for the elderly became segregation of the elderly, and public housing became synonymous with structures in which, as Ciardullo writes in "Urban Housing," "entrances, stairs, and corridors [served] too many people to allow the comforting identification of neighbors and strangers."

Modern technological possibilities had seduced architects into forgetting social scale and consequences. A new 20-story building would abruptly increase the neighborhood population by 200 families, and often times the new families were cultural and ethnic outsiders from some far-away district of the city. This deliberate introduction of a multitude of strangers into a previously intimate neighborhood upset the balance of known to unknown faces.

The architectural form was invasive. Towers presented anonymous façades. Ciardullo recognized that much of the new architecture obliterated vital segments of the continuum, both inside and outside the structures. They stood on vast expanses of public space, which implied the possibility of social interaction within the neighborhood, but in fact discouraged it, because the yards were too large and impersonal for any use. Residents and the surrounding neighbors were deprived of familiar space where they could meet and interact. The three realms of neutral ground–patios or front stoops (private/group); front yards (group); and common play areas (public/group)–in other words, the space that makes us neighbors–belonged to no one group, nor to the city at large.

The open ground at the bases of the high-rises, like the no-man's land stretching between medieval villages, quickly became the locale of muggings and other crimes. Ad hoc patrol groups were a common response, but not an effective one. Graffiti and vandalism were the last resort of individuals reacting to a hostile and homogenizing architectural environment.

Internally as well, these experimental spaces truncated the privacy-to-community continuum. One was expected to move directly from the private/family realm of one's cubbyhole into the public/urban realm of the non-differentiated outdoor space, passing only through an approximation of private/group space: double-loaded corridors and a single entrance, trafficked by near-total strangers who nonetheless lived next door.

This architecture robs its residents of control. With only one entrance, a person cannot choose between two routes. With no private/group space, no yard, and no public/group space, such as a common play area, residents cannot choose to be available for social interaction with their neighbors, nor can they play with their families outside of their own private environment: the allotted apartment. One family cannot choose to associate with another; there is no place to do it.

Every day residents are faced with two opposing positions within the community: in or out. There is nothing in between. These buildings deny residents control over their environment and cause them to lose interest in it. The residents cannot make the environment their own so they absolve themselves of responsibility, ignore the environment, allow it to decay, and even deface it to speed its depreciation.

People need to interact and to be part of a community. But once a community is destroyed by careless architecture and infrastructure, dissipated by vandalized buildings, and decimated by abandoned or poorly planned public spaces, the next architect who is asked to build there must piece together a vision of a community restored to unity. They must construct or reconstruct a physical space that can encourage the members of that community to trust their social environment. Facing the destruction of communities by architecture based only on formal and economic ideals, architects must be sociologists. Their work affects society; they need to know that society.

If any personal characteristics have determined John Ciardullo's approach to architecture and aided his success, particularly in the challenging field of urban, public architecture, they are optimism about society and tenacity in proving himself justified in that optimism. The humanity of Ciardullo's work springs directly from his egalitarian understanding of social status and his belief in the inviolable dignity of each human being. Buildings that don't fit the way the people live, can live, or want to live are quickly abused and abandoned. But the fear of vandalism should not create what Ciardullo terms "a pillbox with a steel door." John Ciardullo Associates' spaces are made "defensible" by positive, rather than negative assumptions; the firm assumes that every individual and every community would rather use its architecture than destroy it. To make it useful is the architect's business.

Public buildings–schools, libraries, community facilities–need most of all to be open. The point of social interaction, or at least the effect, is a reaffirmation of our humanity. When we mix freely, we compare and contrast ourselves with others on a daily basis, and define ourselves within a spectrum of humanity. Public buildings allow people to interact within a preconceived format, for a definitive purpose. But most of our public buildings are designed for another era, when it was more places and reasons to interact. The opportunities for mixing and empathizing have been decreased by every convenience: the car, the highway, the computer. Ciardullo points out that, "in our society today, we live as if the individual were totally alienated from everything." We find our public buildings trapped in their singular functions, and we are loath to visit them. This is how and why we miss out on the excitement of accidental meetings and chance insights. Finally we become dulled to the possibilities of civic life itself.

So, in designing public buildings, the problem is how to allow interaction. Structure is only half of the solution. Programming–the functions assigned by the municipality to a public building–is the other half. From the beginning of a project, the architect-as-sociologist must question programming and advocate possibilities for the entire range of social experiences. In its extensive work with city agencies and school boards, John Ciardullo Associates has found that the original physical assignments can often be improved by including more community-oriented spaces or functions, or by extending the hours of activity. In some cases, politics have slowed progress, but in many, the community has been an active partner to the architect, and programming changes architecture and programming, John Ciardullo Associates has proven many times that a tight site and a small budget do not automatically deny citizens private space, community space, or anything in between.

John Ciardullo's buildings succeed in communities because he sees the existing social organization, respects it, and takes it as a model for the physical form. He knows how strong the community's civic identity is and what forms it has already taken–architecturally and socially. The post office or public pool may be the community's focal point, or there may be none. He understands where people connect, and where they might connect. If the social fabric is intact, the new architecture is simply a rational continuation. If the fabric is damaged, the buildings encourage their repair. If the community is without much of an identity, the building will eventually succeed if it is a shared vision of a new social organization.

John Ciardullo Associates' urban buildings, even those from the mid-1970s, are all still successful, active, and useful, marred with little or no graffiti. In these buildings and their designed external environments, the architect left room for the people. In an active community center, signs of the group's life there–photos, announcements, posters–cover the walls. In his multi-family housing, he has treated each family space separately; residents embellish their doors, lawns, and private gardens with seasonal decorations, family art, and their own choice of plantings, all signs of their identity.

John Ciardullo Associates' designs for planned communities and for private homes have been equally successful as its work in the public sphere. These all-inclusive, ex-urban projects are created for a community that does not yet exist, save in the imaginations of the architect and clients, and perhaps some market research documents. To successfully realize a project that begins as pure potential, the entire plan, infrastructure, siting, materials, and architecture must answer the social and aesthetic expectations of the residents-to-be, offering experiences in every realm of the private-to-community spectrum. These residents, with little or no history in the area, have more choice in their environments than the residents of John Ciardullo Associates' multi-family housing. Abandonment and vandalism are less of a potential problem, but clients for these projects have very specific notions of how they want to interact with their immediate and more distant neighbors, and how their family should feel within the home.

From its earliest efforts, John Ciardullo Associates has built buildings for how we really live, how we interact and how we want to interact. Finally, we see trends supporting the firm's original work: new architecture reaffirming its hard-won victories of social content over architectural form. For instance, at public recreation facilities, libraries, and schools, programming is often changed to reflect our need to communicate and interact in the flesh; both programs and hours of operation are being extended. School auditoriums, libraries, and gymnasiums have become the after-hours property of whole communities. Successful new multi-family housing in under-served communities is by definition low-rise housing with a sense of individual identity. Corporate spaces are flexible environments for productive intra-departmental association; exclusively private cubicles and desks are becoming details of the past. Even within the authority of the municipal architects, the understanding has grown: life must lead architecture.

Community Centers

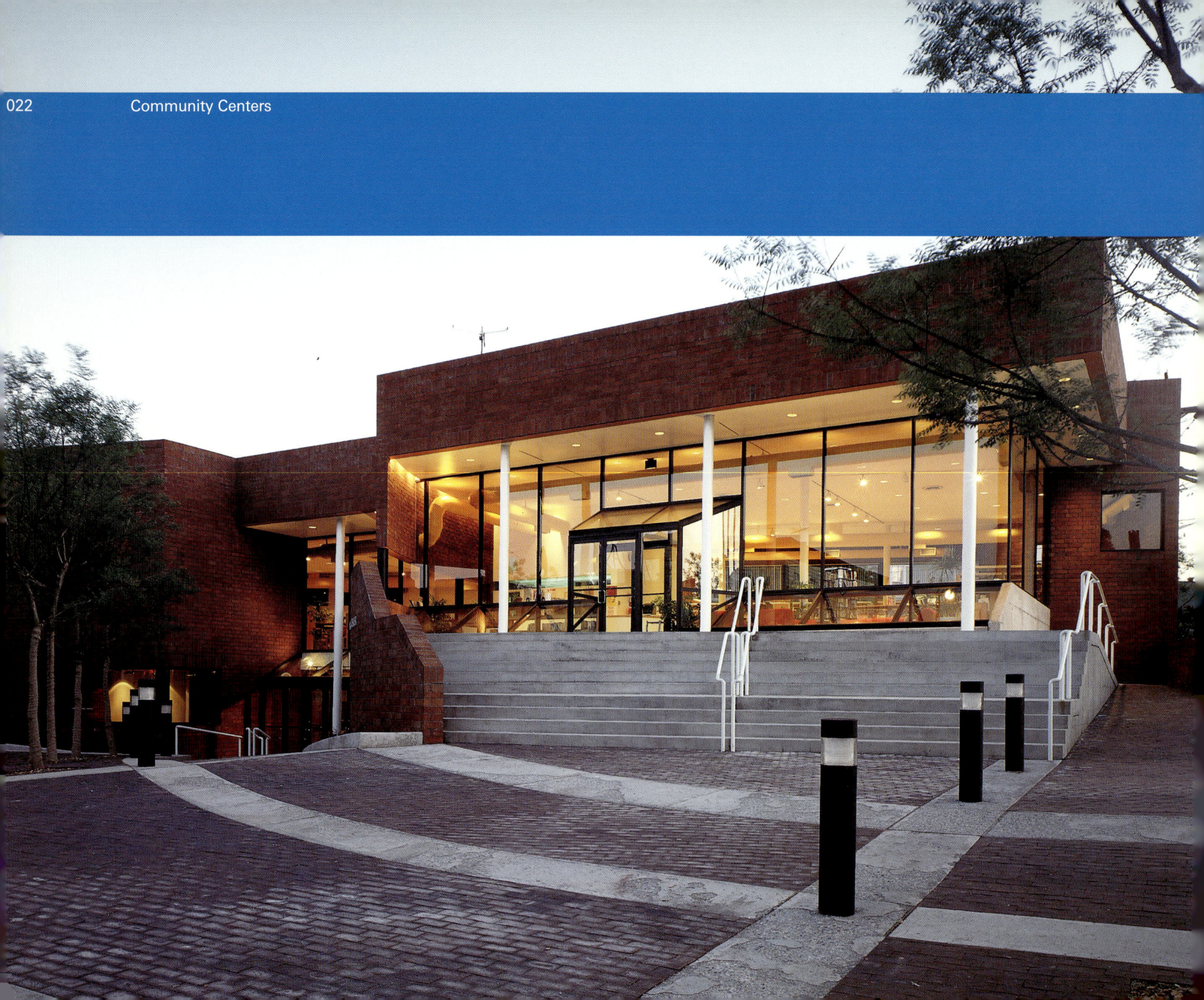

"What is a community? A community is a church or any organization that brings people together to interact because they have something in common. People crave interaction, to be part of something. Even the volunteer fire department is partially a guise for meeting people.

"A community center is the most formalized facility provided by government, which in turn is a formal representation of the community. Its purpose is to provide a function, but also, in doing that, to provide for interaction among different parts of the community, in a formalized way. The architect creates a place where people can meet and interact. If you design something to keep people out, they will break in. If you design for the people, it will give an identity to the entire community. It will survive."

John Ciardullo

Boylan Street Pool
Newark, New Jersey (1975)

The original Boylan Street Pool–a wading pool and Olympic size swimming pool with a bath-house surrounded by a vast plain of concrete paving–was erected in the 1930s. In that era, swimmers would normally change at the pool and spend the day there. The original long, low bath-house was designed to provide such obsolete functions as attendant-manned checking within a contrived symmetrical plan. In 1975, when John Ciardullo Associates accepted this project, funded by the federal, state, and city governments, the physical conditions of the Boylan Street Pool no longer met the social conditions. Bathers would come ready to swim and wanted access to other recreational facilities to make the trip to the pool worthwhile, and the government wanted more for the money it invested.

The pool complex, abutting private property on a quiet residential street, had also become a rendezvous spot for troublemaking teenagers. To discourage these uncivil gatherings and encourage year-round use of the space, John Ciardullo Associates suggested the city acquire a small piece of land facing a busy commercial street. The architects then closed off the original entrance and reordered traffic through a modest entrance on the side of the commercial street, which helped define a radically different use of the site while keeping the stable residential character of the community. Visitors now enter from this more appropriately public zone, passing through a progressively diminishing plaza dotted with a grid pattern of trees.

A new wing projects off the original building at an angle, enclosing the site and giving visitors a sense of both protection and relaxation. The architects matched the original brick and retained charming features like the semi-circular, half-height brick walls as well as the hand-washing basins, but replaced the large changing rooms with small spaces for quieter pursuits and allowed larger areas for active play. The architects added colorful exposed spiral ducts to reiterate the friendly character of this mature community facility. To delineate the entrance and allow for control and casual surveillance, the architects added walls and gates as well. There is also an angled office-meeting room addition, where staff can monitor the entrance and visitors can relax and enjoy an expansive view. Outside, new multi-level platforms and landscaping inexpensively enhance visitors' physical and social experience of the pool complex.

In this rehabilitation of a seasonal bath-house and pool into a year-round indoor/outdoor facility for every age group, John Ciardullo Associates maintained the positive, neighborly aspects of the community facility, but added enough non-specific space to allow for changing recreational needs. At the time of its construction, the new wing provided room for community meetings, wrestling, weight lifting, billiards, a library, and an after-school program for children.

Facing page:
Axonometric

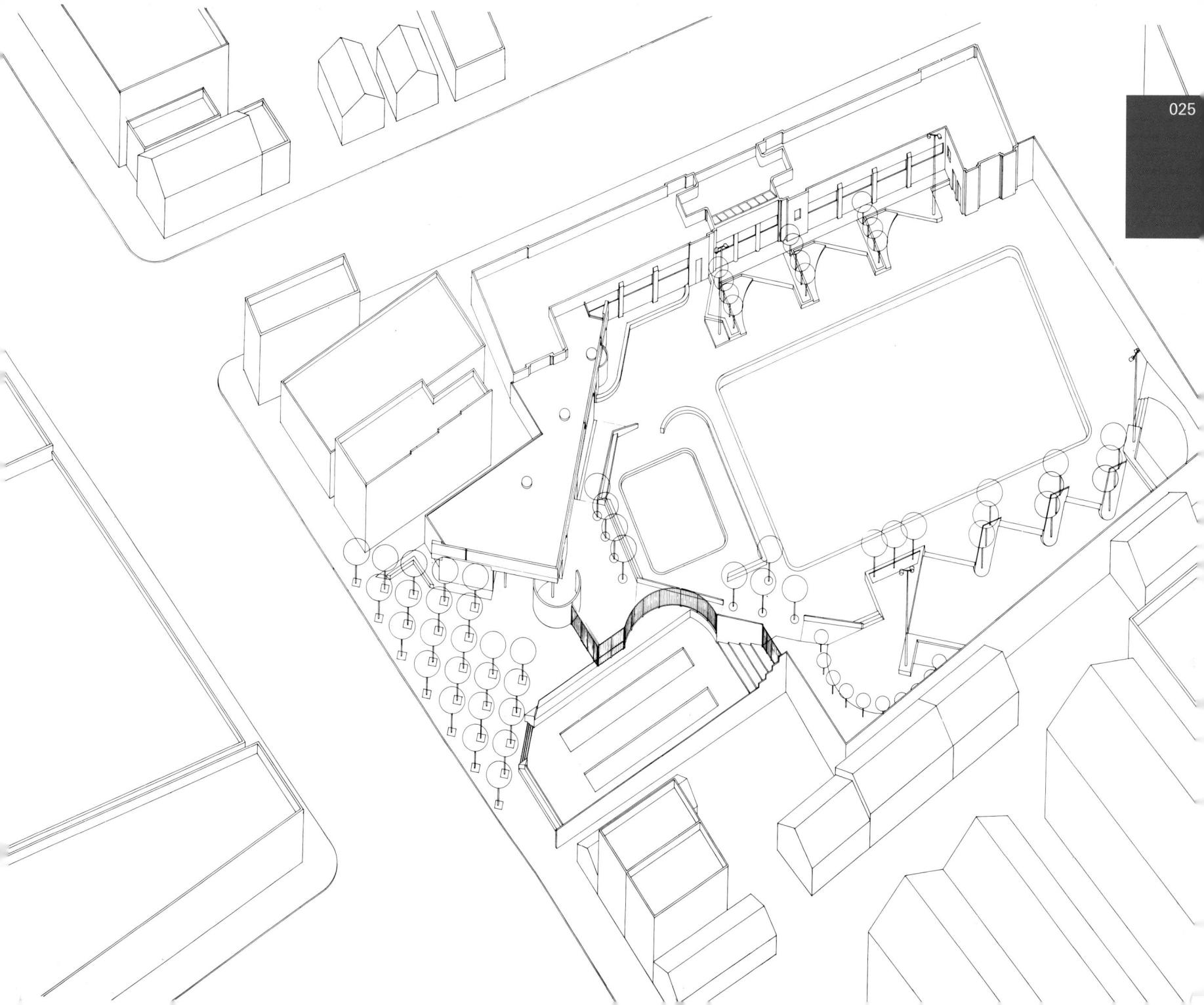

025

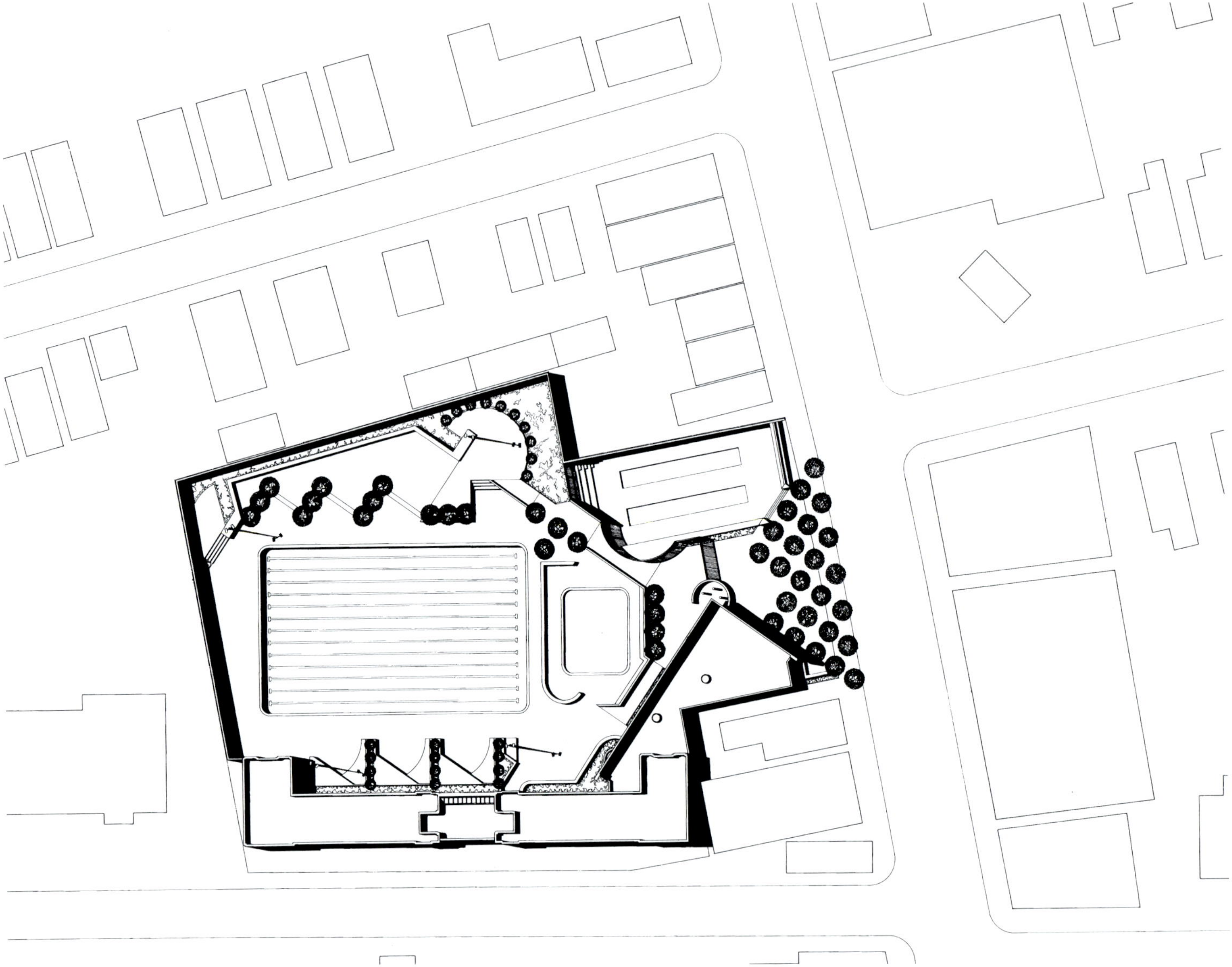

026

Drawing:
Site plan

Facing page:
Multi-level platforms and landscaping enhance the experience of the pool area.

027

Above left:
Colorful, exposed spiral ducts in the corridor create a friendly character.

Above right:
The semi-circular form of the entry desk is repeated throughout the complex.

Below:
The manager's office opens to the pool area.

Facing page:
The half-height, semi-circular wall contains outdoor showers.

030

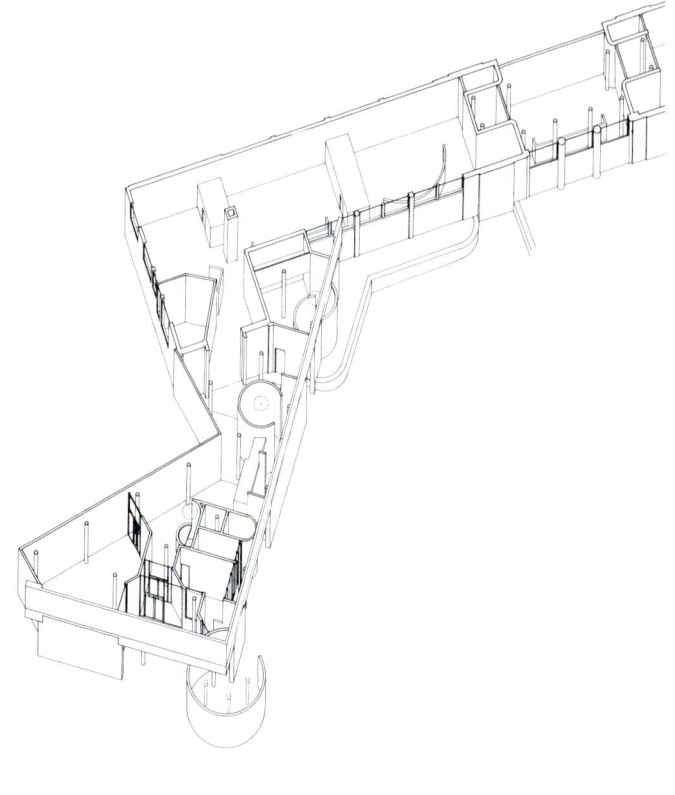

Above:
The entrance plaza is dotted with a soothing grid pattern of trees.

Drawing:
Axonometric of addition

Facing page:
From the pool area, the recreation building creates a transition to the neighborhood.

031

St. Peter's Park and Recreation Center
Newark, New Jersey (1976)

Using a simple triangular shape and the inviting aspect of open space, John Ciardullo Associates revived a previously lifeless park, thus inspiring the residents of this low-income neighborhood in Newark, New Jersey to visit their park, to use it, and to make it their own.

Early on, this project proved that analysis of the real needs and desires of a community could lead to a building that would engage users in its variety, even while adhering to budget and design constraints. Previous to the architects' evaluation of the real social needs and patterns, the defunct St. Peter's Park had motivated people only to vandalism. John Ciardullo Associates proposed that the municipality offer more recreation for more hours per day, or in other words, discourage destruction by encouraging activity. The master plan consolidates a community center, a branch library, a multipurpose space, a social service office, a health center, and two outdoor pools in addition to the existing basketball courts and baseball fields.

The social purpose of the project was to encourage the community's dynamic interaction. The architects achieved this with several physical solutions. A single path leading to all of the activity areas brings people in contact with one another whether they are heading for the pools or the pavilion. The pavilion is a triangular form that intentionally meets the path at the corner to visually and physically anchor the entire park and draw in community members.

The ground floor houses washrooms and changing rooms for the outdoor pools, granting immediate use of the facility. The second, or mezzanine level encourages more quiet pursuits. It includes a small snack bar and overlooks a very active, public, multi-functional space. A protruding ramp, with its sculptural form, functionally and visually connects the two levels.

While many community centers in low-income neighborhoods have been constructed as veritable locked boxes, barred and shuttered to protect them from supposedly destructive individuals, the exact opposite tack has been taken by John Ciardullo Associates. The architects opened the building visually with a transparent curtainwall that ever so lightly defines the boundary between inside and outside. This wall invites every member of the community to either enter or watch the activity from the outdoor semicircular terrace, which extends through the wall from the interior mezzanine level.

In contrast to the glass wall, the two remaining sides of the triangle present a solid and reliable façade of brick masonry. These physically shield the building from southern exposure, structurally support floor and roof systems, and visually anchor the back corner of the building. The pool appears to be one with the lawn, due to a double stainless steel surge wall and a deck level overflow system. The effect is an even more generous visual plane.

St. Peter's Park and Recreation Center integrates the physical with the social response to a particular community's needs. It makes community a function of the architecture. The fact that it has remained in excellent condition for many years proves that the people who use it consider it their own.

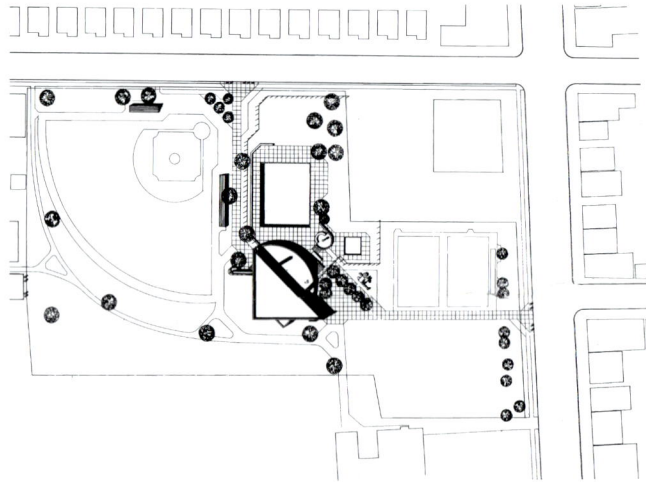

Facing page:
The recreation center's transparent curtainwall ever so lightly defines the boundary between inside and out.

Drawing:
Site plan

034

035

Facing page:
The pool and lawn areas merge to create one continuous space.

Above:
The mezzanine's balcony overlooks the recreation area.

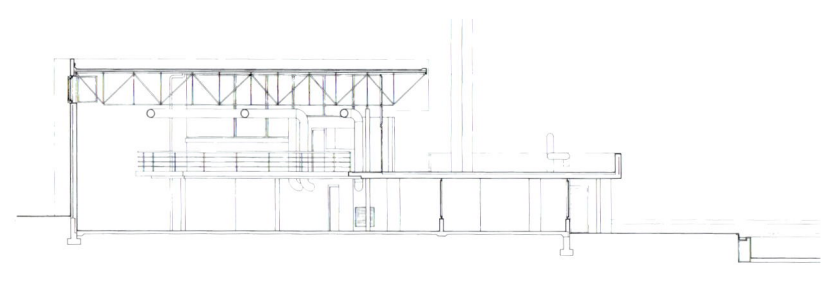

Drawing:
Section

Above:
The terrace and snack bar provide a place for more quiet pursuits.

Facing page:
In form the entrance to the recreation building is open to the rest of the site.

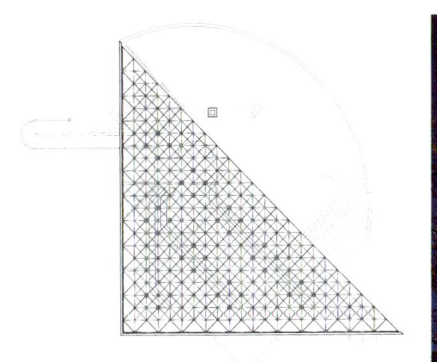

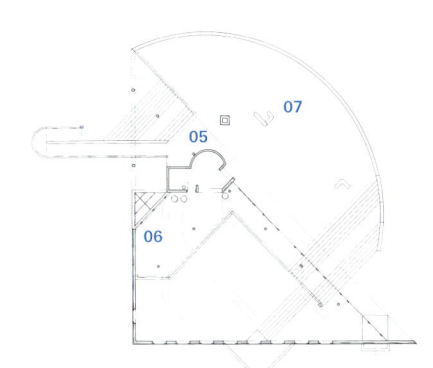

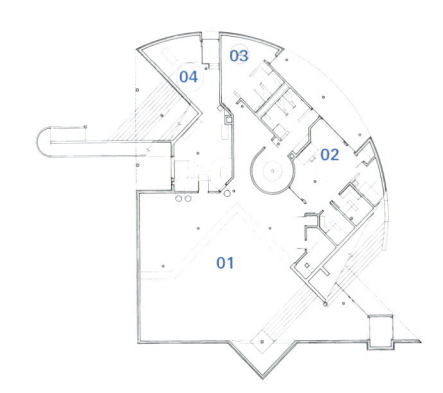

01.
Recreation area

02.
Women's locker room

03.
Men's locker room

04.
Mechanical room

05.
Snack bar

06.
Balcony

07.
Terrace

Drawings bottom to top: Entry, plaza, and roof level plans.

038

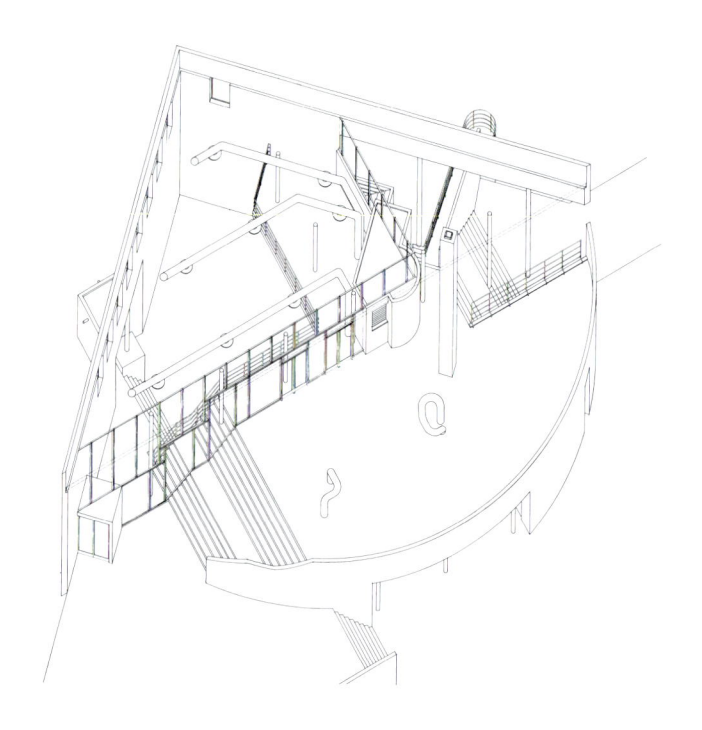

Above:
From inside there are direct views to the surrounding neighborhood.

Drawing:
Axonometric

Facing page:
The sculptural form of the protruding ramp visually and functionally connects the building's two levels.

039

South Paterson Public Library
Paterson, New Jersey (1978)

South Paterson Public Library gave John Ciardullo Associates the chance to integrate John Ciardullo's ideas on extended hours and programming, which envision community as a function of the architecture. For many years the library on this site had existed only as a storefront facility, constraining the community with its limited size, layout, and programming. Encouraged by the architects, the city determined that the community needed a more broadly functional facility than could be provided by a typical branch library.

Today the library is a physical manifestation of the complex needs of an urban community, summoning the public to partake of the entire range of activities, from reading privately to obtaining public services. In addition to an elderly day care center, the building accommodates facilities for police community relations, ambulance services, community meetings, and library-related programs. Although the budget was nominal, John Ciardullo Associates assured the community's satisfaction.

As the architects attempted to satisfy the various needs and functions of the program, they were first challenged by the site itself. The structure is prominently located at the intersection of five commercial and residential streets. To integrate a small traffic island into a pedestrian-friendly piazza, the architects closed a minor through street. This consequently brought the tip of the site out into the street, indicating the relationship between the building and the community and acknowledging the existing social context. The forecourt is alternately paved and landscaped, creating both an inviting extended entrance and a nearly public park for repose–an open space of refuge along the busy thoroughfare.

The building mass and volumes growing up out of the site relate directly to the scale of the existing neighborhood. The architects rotated the front elevation and entrance to be parallel with the main street. This established a connection between the library and community traffic. At the same time, the unique rounded shape of the piazza buffered the library from the street's linear emphasis on movement. The gesture of the curving wall, which bisects the building vertically, embraces the neighborhood and leads patrons to either the upper or lower level.

The architects separated the facility's functions by floor. They provided two equally prominent entrances: the lower leads into the community spaces and the upper is used by library visitors. Visitors enter the first floor directly below a glass wall on the second, and are thus immediately aware of the building's dual function. Likewise, from the library, patrons can look down on the first-floor intersection of the curved wall and façade.

Details devised to solve spatial limits include the exposed and brightly painted tubes of the heating system, which were located along the periphery of the space in order to gain as much ceiling height as possible. The main entrance allows natural light to illuminate the reading rooms and community room. Skylights improve the lighting of the subterranean meeting room, as does a horizontal strip of windows situated just above ground level on the south side of the building. The children's area is sunken one step below the general reading area and is bordered by the curving wall. The building has aged elegantly, thanks to the architects' choice of materials: brick walls, metal decking floors, and steel columns and beams. Built a quarter century ago, the South Paterson Library and Community Center has not suffered broken windows or graffiti and is still a magnificent, highly used facility, treated as a respected civic institution and a place of knowledge. It continues to stand as a valued home for the community.

Facing page:
The glass curtain-wall of the library entrance is on the second floor.

041

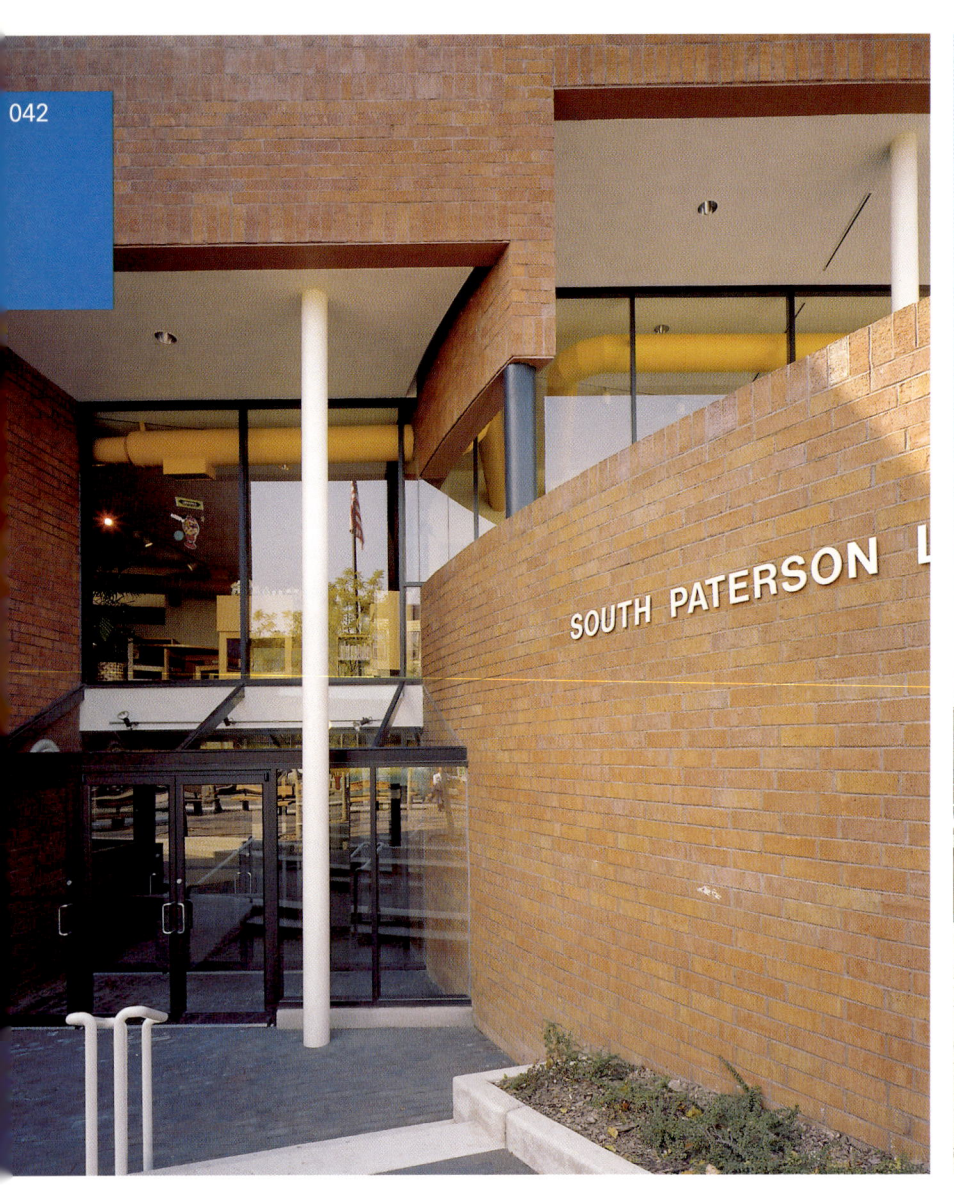

Above left:
The first floor entrance leads to a meeting room and police auxiliary office.

Above right:
Stairs and a ramp lead up to the library level.

043

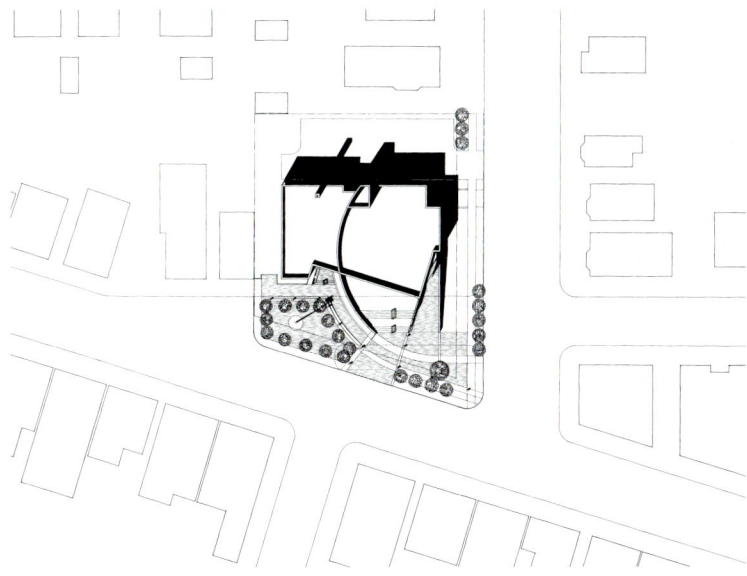

Drawing:
Site plan

Above:
The library entrance is set parallel to the street.

044

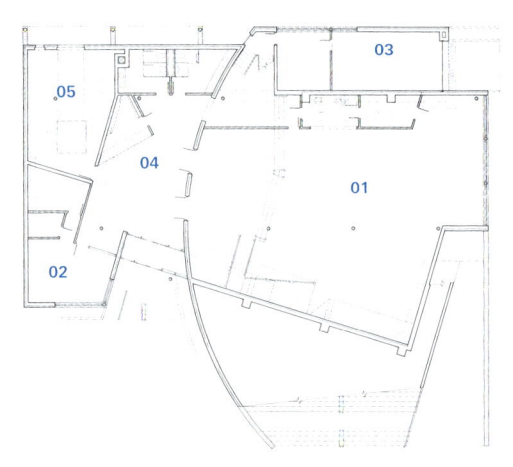

01.
Meeting room

02.
Police auxiliary office

03.
Ambulance

04.
Lower lobby

05.
Mechanical room

Above:
The raised library entrance provides a perch from which to view the neighborhood.

Drawing:
Lower level plan

045

Above left:
The curving brick wall breaks up the linear relationship between site and street.

Above right:
Skylights help illuminate the subterranean meeting room.

046

047

01.
Main reading room

02.
Children's reading room

03.
Circulation desk

04.
Office

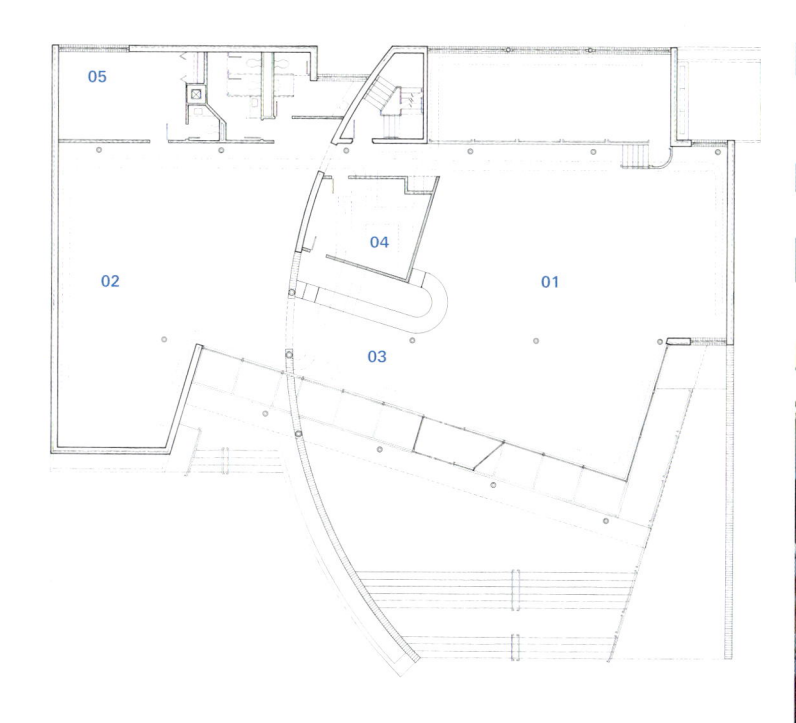

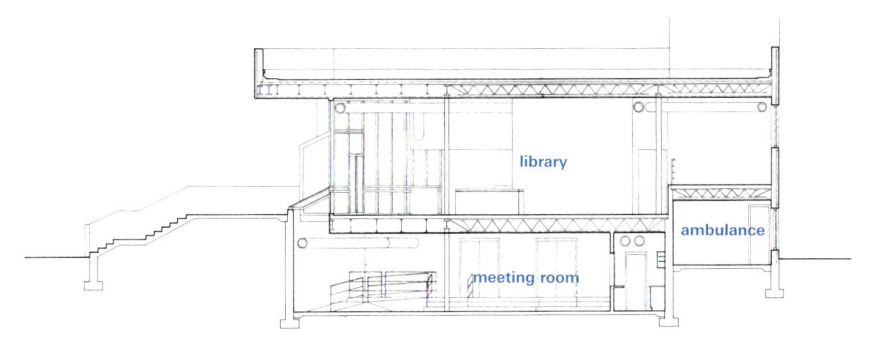

05.
Workroom

Facing page:
The glass curtain-wall allows natural light to flood the main reading room and circulation desk.

Drawing above:
Library level plan

Above:
Views are open from the children's reading room to the main reading room and the street.

Drawing below:
Section

Owen Dolen Golden Age Center
Bronx, New York (1982)

The Owen Dolen Golden Age Center, housed in a turn-of-the-century two-story library on a triangle of land on Westchester Square, was too small for the growing elderly community in the Southeast Bronx. No solution was immediately apparent. The program required an addition of equal size, 2,500 square feet, but any proposed structure had to maintain the historic building, its pleasant social context, the existing park, and its public access, while also providing some small portion of outdoor space specifically for the elderly who use the center. The site itself is in one of the most public locations in the area–a square, surrounded on three sides by busy streets and bounded by public sidewalks, where buses and elevated trains stop, discharging and accepting passengers.

Although it was not large enough for its clientele, the facility already exhibited a fine balance with the surrounding community. To maintain that balance as well as the physical characteristics of the site, John Ciardullo Associates extended the facility underground. A partially submerged structure containing a multipurpose room, a kitchen, and handicapped bathrooms stretches under the raised public plaza, which is level with the arched windows on the existing building.

The architects kept the deck as thin as possible by using flat plate cast-in-place concrete, which is also extremely durable and fire resistant. The project received the 1983 Concrete Industry Board award for innovative use of concrete in the cultural building category. Sculptural steel pipes, playful elements both inside and out, are the intakes and exhausts for fresh air and air conditioning equipment.

At the far end of the park, the addition emerges as a decidedly modern, contrasting sculptural element, a large, sandblasted concrete triangle announcing the new entrance. A five-tier recirculating fountain, connecting the upper and lower reflecting pools, animates the jutting triangle. This element also brings natural light into the addition, effectively connecting it with the outdoor space.

Although most of the addition is underground, the innovative use of each possible aperture connects it to the existing structure and the outdoor space, all of which are available to the elderly community. Inside, the straight bold lines of the varied windows contrast with the original half-moon clerestory windows in the multipurpose room and point the way to the newly created semi-private park for the elderly. Ramps and handicapped facilities are evident throughout the design.

From the sidewalk, level with the entrance to the original structure, members of the community at large enter the public plaza by climbing a set of stairs flanking the building and the earth berm that insulates the addition. Architecturally, the addition claims its own identity, increasing the significance of the older building by initiating a dialogue with it. The senior citizen community of the Bronx has embraced the redefined center.

Facing page:
The asymmetrical addition decidedly contrasts the original facility.

049

Above:
The addition opens from the meeting space to a private outdoor sitting area.

051

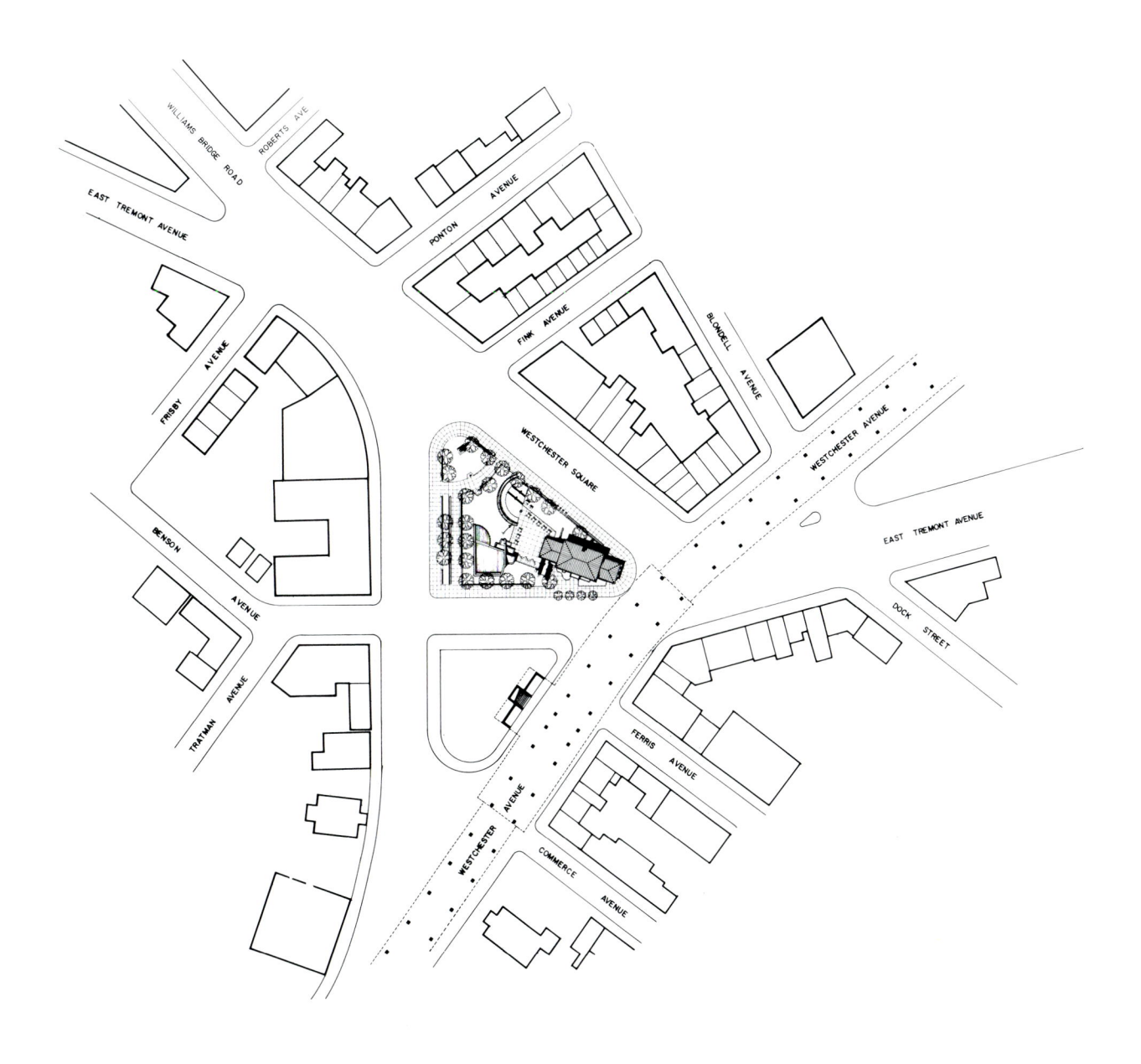

Drawing:
Site plan

052

053

01.
Meeting room

02.
Entrance

03.
Foyer

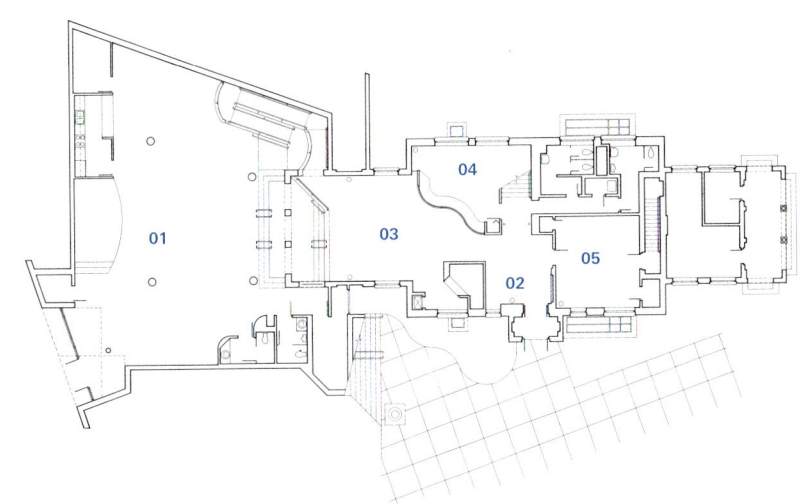

04.
Office

05.
Recreation room

Facing page:
The foyer and office transition from the original building to the addition.

Above left:
The meeting room in the addition is submerged beneath a public sitting area.

Above right:
Before descending into the meeting room, high windows in the foyer bring in natural light.

Drawing:
Lower level plan

054

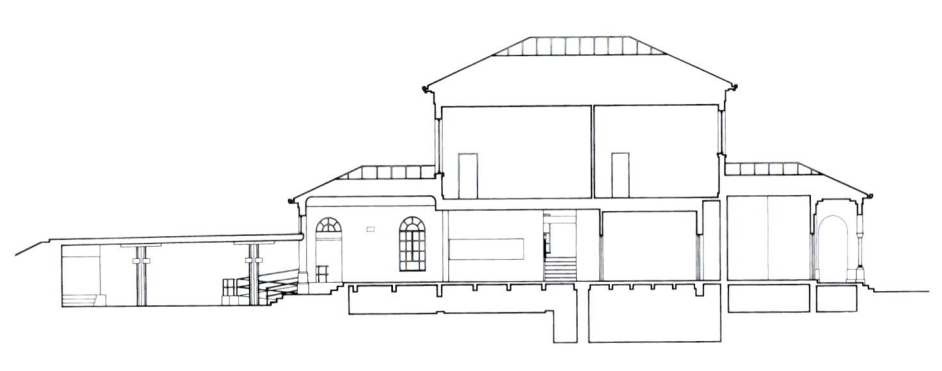

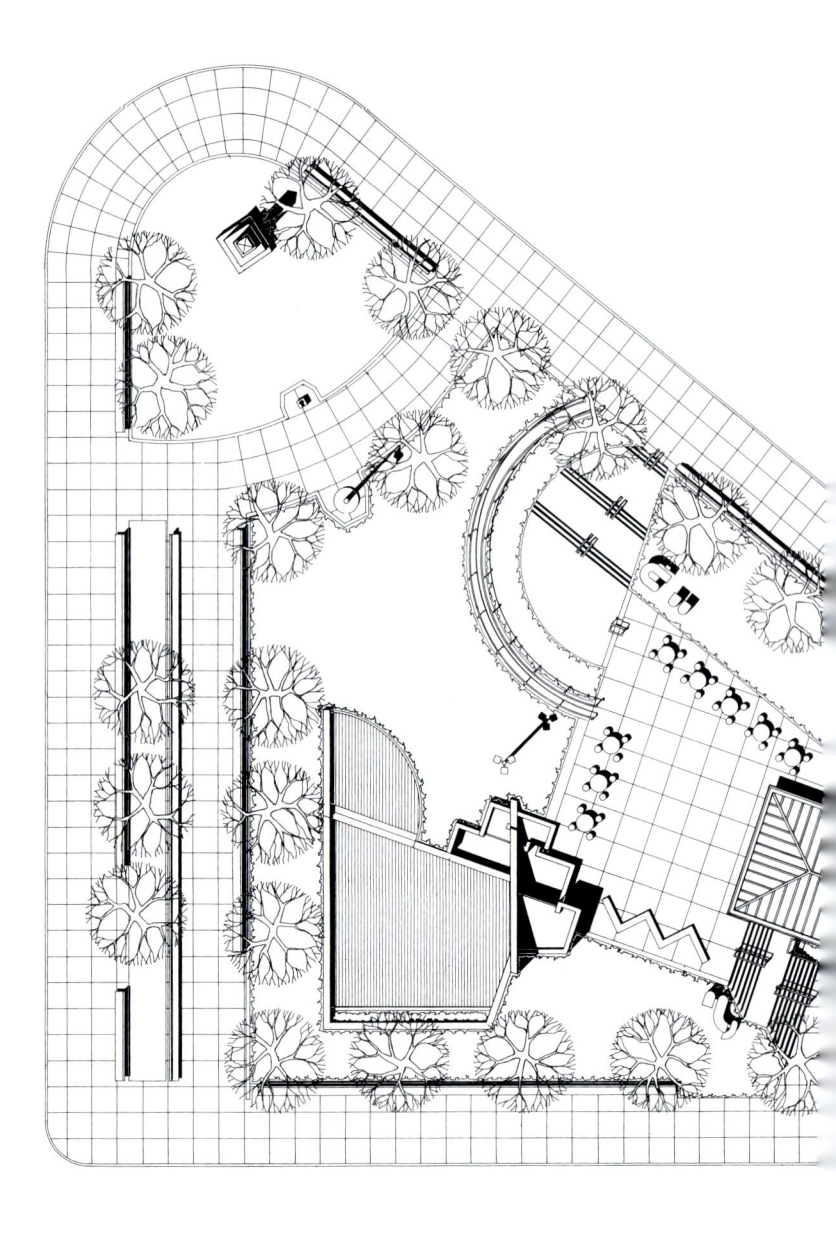

Above:
A five-tier, re-circulating water fall animates the meeting room exterior.

Drawing above:
Longitudinal section

Drawing center:
Site plan

055

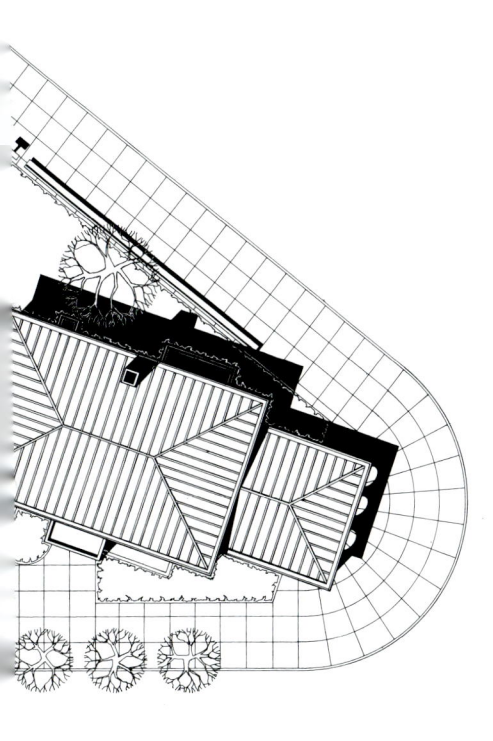

Above:
Steps ascend to
a public sitting
area above the
submerged addition.

Isabelle Miller Community Center
Camden, New Jersey (1982)

The Isabelle Miller Community Center in Camden, New Jersey was composed of a vandalized 50-year-old pool/bath house facility on a one-acre site and a ten-year-old athletic complex on a separate 12-acre site. John Ciardullo Associates transformed the center into a venue for recreation and community services, operating with a full-time staff all year round. Before beginning work on this project, the architects performed a study and conferred with the appropriate city officials to determine how the space could most effectively involve the whole community. At their suggestion, disparate departments of the local government, each of which sought space for various services, joined forces in this project. After demolishing the existing pool complex and converting the one-acre site into a children's park, John Ciardullo Associates consolidated the year-round recreational activities into one facility on the 12-acre site. Twenty years after its construction, the facility remains well maintained, and an important locus for the community.

The new facility includes swimming, diving, and wading pools and a community building that holds a branch library, a social services center, a Deputy Mayor's annex, and a community meeting room. In a second phase, John Ciardullo Associates designed a one-story addition for use as a health center, which was sorely needed by the community.

The neighborhood of the Isabelle Miller Community Center is made up of low-income public housing projects. The challenge of the project was to create a unified cohesive building where anyone could participate in a number of diverse and unrelated activities. To make the complex a focal point for the community, the architects created a number of entrances and unified them through placement. Diagonal to a street corner, the complex presents a landscaped public plaza as a physical first word in the discourse between the architecture and its community. Those who choose to enter the complex on the ground level will walk between the rounded masonry wall of the community center and the rectilinear masonry wall of the health center, proceeding through a short "tunnel" that opens onto the generous outdoor pool complex.

Visitors who need or choose to enter the complex via the elongated ramp, which reaches from the street corner, arrive in front of a second-level interior window overlooking the pools. From here, patrons can keep visual track of others in their party while en route to the second-floor library, Deputy Mayor's office, or Youth Services office. An interior staircase leads to the same second-floor balcony, which, from the other side, looks down on the community room below. The terracing of the pools refers visually to this open, stepping interior organization and inspires in the visitor a sense of the variety of purpose and function maintained in the complex, without unduly isolating any activity or person.

The consolidation of communal and social activities, carried on for 16 hours each day, creates a true community center and fosters a strong sense of collective identity.

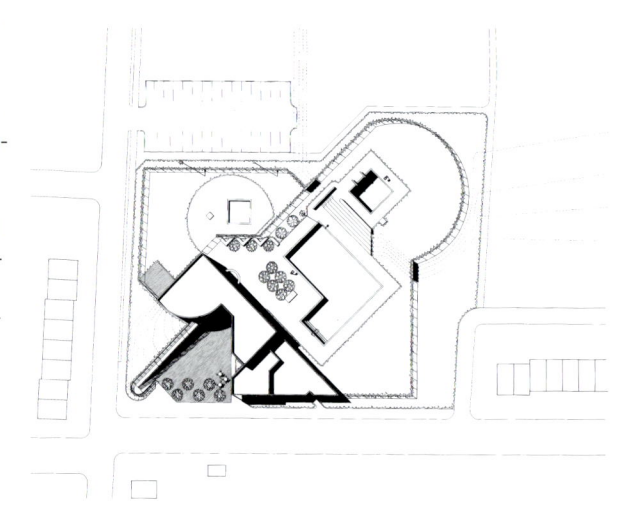

Facing page:
Entrances are provided for direct access to the pool, social service office, library, or health care center.

Drawing:
Site plan

057

058

Left:
An aperture in the community building provides free access to the pool area.

Center:
The pool area is clearly visible from the second floor of the community building.

059

Right:
Separate diving
and lap pools are
available.

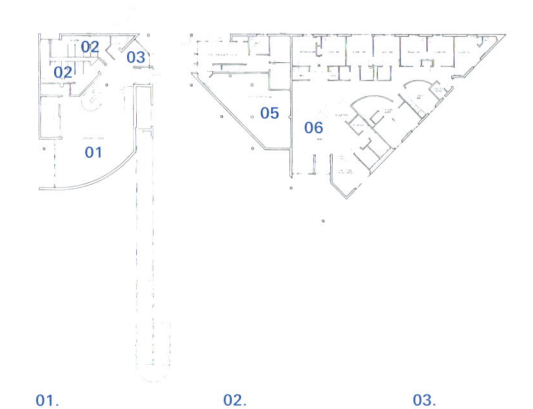

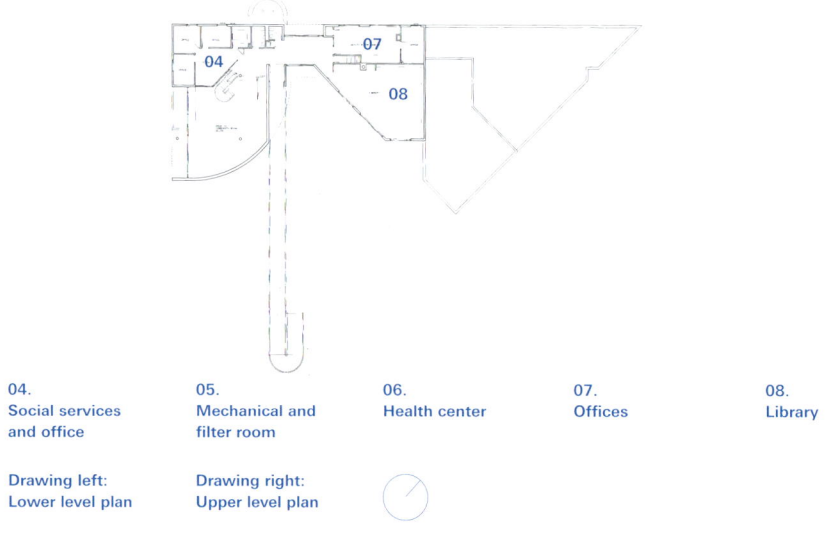

01.
Meeting room
and kitchen

02.
Toilets

03.
Entry to meeting
room

04.
Social services
and office

05.
Mechanical and
filter room

06.
Health center

07.
Offices

08.
Library

Above Left:
The meeting room
is directly accessible from the pool
area.

Above right:
A stair links the
second story to the
meeting room.

Drawing left:
Lower level plan

Drawing right:
Upper level plan

061

Above:
The meeting room features its own entrances, one to the plaza and one to the pool area.

062

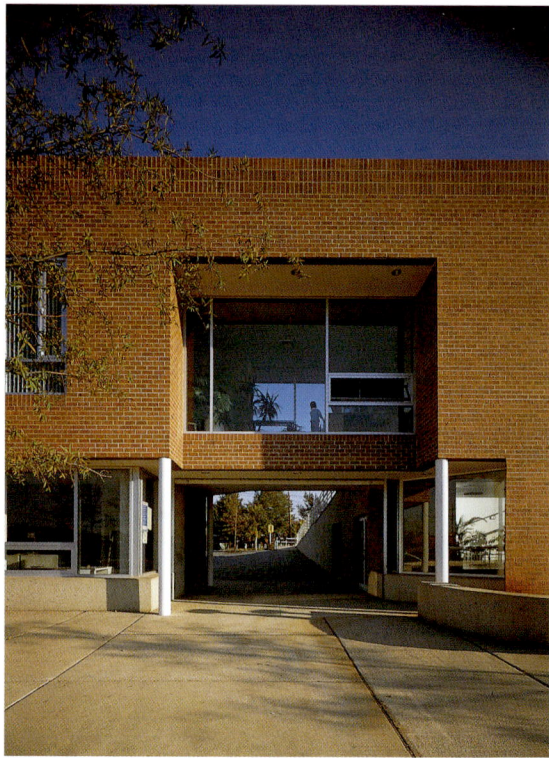

Above left:
The second floor library offers a quiet place to read.

Above right:
From the pool area, the entry plaza is visible.

063

Above:
The neighborhood can be seen from the second floor.

Hamilton Fish Park and Recreation Center
New York, New York (1992)

Named in honor of a past Secretary of State (c. 1869-1877), Hamilton Fish Park and Recreation Center is a triumph of social architecture, balancing a respect for history with the principles of modern design. John Ciardullo Associates was honored to restore this elegant Carrere and Hastings structure, which was inspired by the 1895 Petit Palais in Paris and erected in 1902 on a four-acre site of Lower East Side tenement housing. The architects considered the neighborhood first, the social situation and the habits of prospective patrons. Then they repositioned the boundaries of the site and the entrances to provide security and a sense of belonging. Finally, they suggested reprogramming that would make the complex a year-round facility attractive to all members of the community. The materials chosen, from simple brick to wrought iron, mahogany, terazzo, and marble, reinforced John Ciardullo's primary belief that if a building is both useful and beautiful, people will take care of it. Although John Ciardullo Associates and the community were in agreement on this point from the beginning, a decade passed before the city abandoned its argument of fortifying a structure against vandalism, rather than opening it to enjoyment.

John Ciardullo Associates received a number of awards for its work, including the American Institute of Architects New York Chapter 1994 Architecture Award and The City Club of New York's 28th Bard Award for Excellence in Architecture and Urban Design 1995. Shortly after the Center reopened, the *New York Times* architecture critic Herbert Muschamp wrote, "The water in Fish Park's pools has bubbled up from some of the deepest wells in New York's social and architectural history. It is…a powerful tonic against despair." The state of the site when it was closed because of neglect and an outdated plan was indeed cause for despair. The complex had originated as a lovely example of the Beaux-Arts style, but from the beginning failed to meet the local immigrant community's needs. It was redesigned and reopened in 1905 with an outdoor track, and tennis and basketball courts, and remained in use until 1936, the beginning of Robert Moses' tenure as Parks Commissioner. Moses advanced Aymer Embury's design of two fenced-in pools and a reprogrammed gym. The newly designed park functioned for 52 years.

Embury's plan, however, allowed patrons to enter the park without entering the facility proper, so that over the years the park became a favorite spot for unscrupulous activities; pool users were swimming over broken glass bottles and graffiti scarred the pool walls. The facility's filtration systems were outdated, its roofs dilapidated, windows broken or blocked, woodwork rotted and the original masonry, lacking insulation, was also buried under layers of paint. Needless to say, because the facility was built in 1936, wheelchair access was also limited. In these more litigious times, the entire facility had become a liability.

John Ciardullo Associates took the neighborhood's needs and desires into account and delivered a master plan that redefined the facility, which had become a burden on the community, as a center of the community. The social model necessitated year-round use of a secure piece of real estate with facilities that were pleasant to visit and use. Perimeter fences were installed around the entire park, thus controlling the entrance and defining the boundary between public and semi-public space. Original trees were retained and incorporated into the reclaimed park, where visitors can spend the day on handball or basketball courts and kids can amuse themselves in the playground, which is paved with recycled tires. The semi-circular pool is now a shallow training pool and the larger pool meets Olympic standards. A new stainless steel high-rate filtration system serves both pools through an access tunnel. The brick masonry around the pool relates to the exterior of the building, the original limestone and brick, which were cleansed of graffiti. The architects insisted on high-quality, low-maintenance, efficient materials: insulated walls clad in marble, a terrazzo floor, and mahogany woodwork to replace the pine of the 1936 remodeling. The gymnasium now has a new life as a community center with meeting rooms, classrooms, and a theater stage. It serves local boys' clubs, community service groups, and individuals who use it for special events, such as wedding receptions. From the beginning, John Ciardullo Associates did not consider Hamilton Fish Park and Recreation Center as a historical building to restore, but as an opportunity to manifest a changing community in a piece of historically meaningful architecture. In over a

Facing page:
The Hamilton Fish Park is an appealing oasis in its ultra-urban context.

065

decade of constant use (75 to 80 children participate in the after-school program every day, and during the summer 85,000 swimmers visit the pool) the Center has remained attractive to the members of this multi-ethnic community, in great part because it is beautiful and safe. They have made Hamilton Fish Park and Recreation Center a valued locus for their community activities.

Above:
Prior to renovation the community building was in a dilapidated state.

Below:
The Beaux-Arts style façade of the community building stands out against the neighboring housing complexes.

Facing page:
The original trees were maintained in the sitting area adjacent to the pool.

067

Left:
Inside the meeting room such materials as terrazzo floors, and marble walls, make for a high-quality, yet low-maintenance space.

Middle:
Stairs leading to a raised terrace above the filter building afford a view of the pool and community building.

Right:
Lobby

069

070

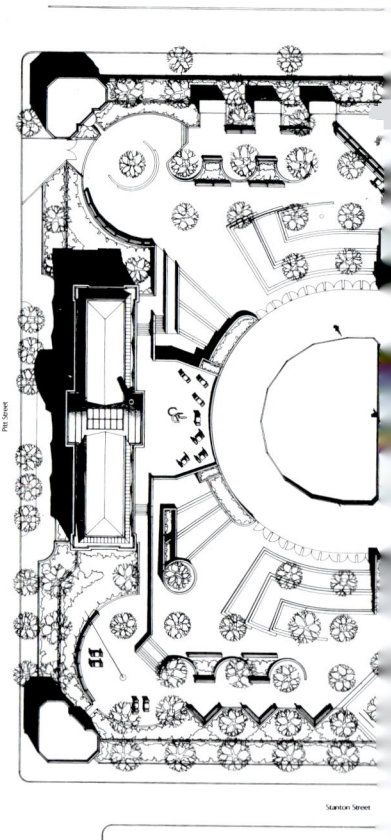

Above:
The community building is clearly visible from the center of the pool.

Drawing:
Site plan

071

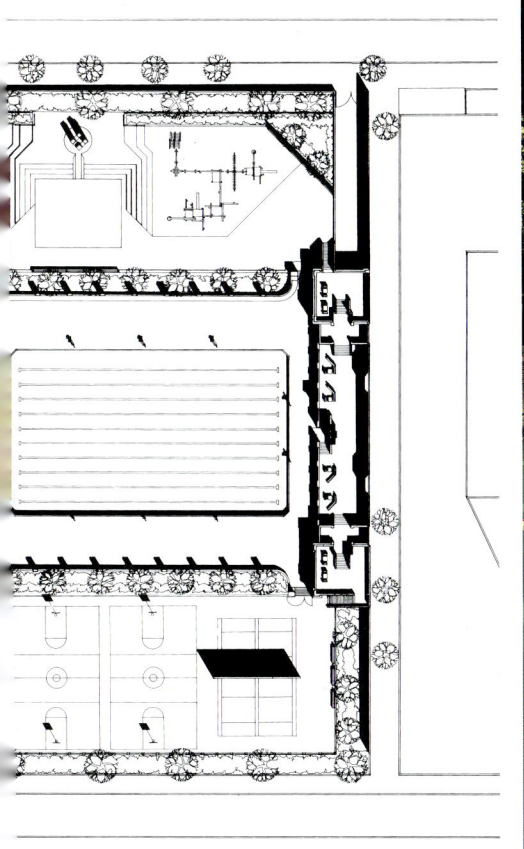

Above:
The filter building and raised terrace anchor the far end of the Olympic sized pool.

Gerritsen Beach Branch Library
Brooklyn, New York (1997)

While designing Gerritsen Beach Branch Library, John Ciardullo Associates confronted the tradition of defensive architecture that had defined the urban library as a dark, cramped building fortified with barred windows and steel shutters to protect against a violent public. After years of lobbying, a South Central Brooklyn community was finally provided a light and spacious library that connects the inner and outer environments. The library established a new community focus that is beloved by its patrons, including students who meet there after school, a habit unimaginable before this building became their library.

The library is situated on Gerritsen Avenue, the area's thoroughfare, which is lined with churches, stores, and a school that determined both the scale of the library and its material palette. Across the street from the Marine Park wildlife habitat, a landscape of marshes, saw grass, and estuaries, and at the head of the Shell Bank Canal, which empties into Sheepshead Bay and harbors the neighborhood pleasure boats, the library's location is dignified and picturesque. The building's arched masonry entrance, which continues as a peaked ceiling through the interior to a full-story window wall, creates a visual link between the park and canal.

The arched masonry entrance also signifies the library's public orientation. It steps back from the street into a vestibule, opening into a landscaped outdoor reading garden on one side and a meeting room, service entrance, and work room on the other. These supporting spaces can be closed off for additional programming outside of library hours. Open for more hours and for a greater variety of purposes than is common for libraries, Gerritsen Beach Branch Library further unifies the community and effectively polices itself.

Walking through the vestibule, patrons are greeted by the soaring space of the public reading room, where the peaked ceiling and full-story window wall frame a view of the canal. Allowing generous streams of natural light into the space, this window links the straight open line of the canal with the stacks and reading tables that align with it. The exterior materials, brick, cast stone, and aluminum, are appropriate to the architectural context and the environment, and continue throughout the interior, unifying the structure and reducing maintenance costs. Heavy, interlocking timber trusses, hung with pendant lights and oriented along the canal axis, support the roof structure and, spanning the full depth of the library, dramatize the reading room spaces. The trusses are in turn supported by round, flanged steel columns set into bases encased with brick and capped with cast stone. The material elements refer visually to the environment of the canal and the docks beyond; trusses recall the wood of the docks, and the brick columns, the piers outside. The spaces created by these vertical elements are semi-private window seats flanked by bookshelves.

The library supports a range of different experiences: the act of reading is intensely private; searching through a library is a more public act–a way to commune with the collective life of the mind; joining in community gatherings is our most public behavior. The outdoor reading garden, visible from the interior through a curving glass wall, creates a palpable membrane that protects the privacy of readers from the public street. The children's reading area, bounded on three sides, gives kids a taste of the semi-private experience of reading with others. The overhang for this garden, supported by trusses that extend through the glass, responds visually to the surrounding neighborhood roofs, reinforcing the fact that a library accepts everyone.

John Ciardullo Associates began this project with a mandate for a 7,500-square-foot space. The firm convinced the client to expand the library to 10,000 square feet, and to put enough glass in the building to make it an enjoyable environment, not just a functional one. As Mayor Rudolph Giuliani said when the library opened, Gerritsen Beach Branch Library is the antithesis of libraries of the past; far from being dark and foreboding, this library is inspired by endless streams of natural light and a clear and pleasant view.

Facing page:
The rear of the library faces Shell Bank Canal.

073

074

075

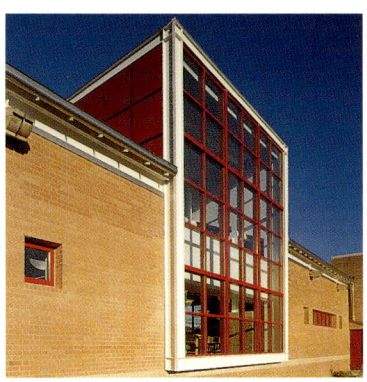

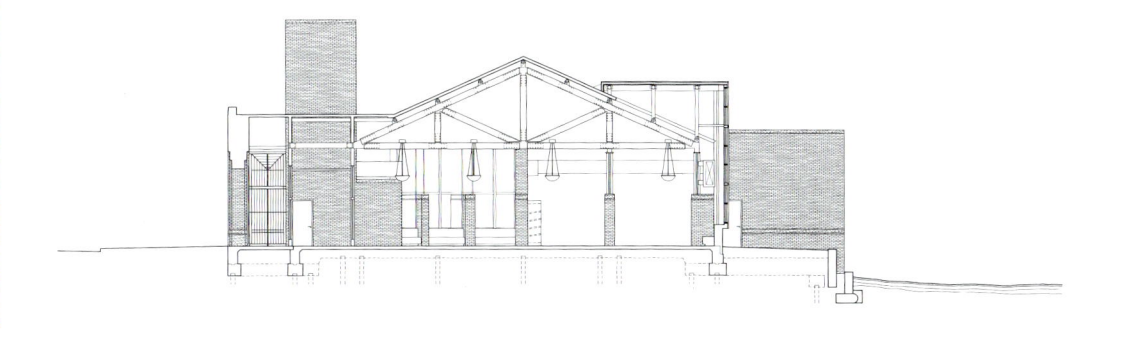

Facing page:
The view passes from the main entry through the library and out the rear window to the canal.

Above:
The floor to ceiling glass curtainwall floods the main reading room with natural light.

Below:
The size of the glass curtainwall was exaggerated to bring in more light.

Drawing:
Transverse section

076

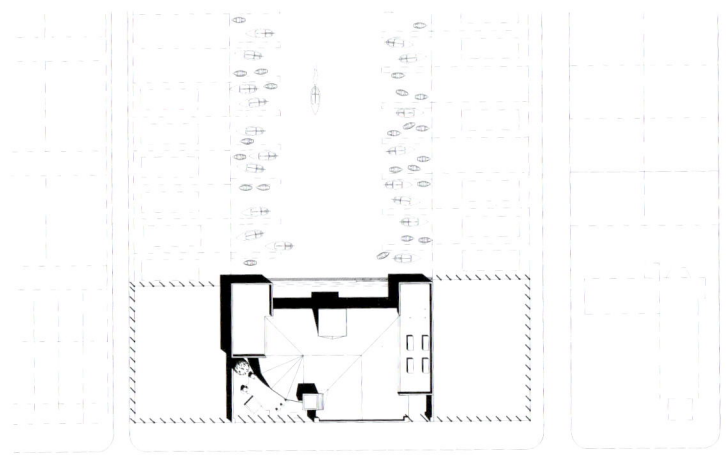

Above:
The children's reading area is visible from the garden.

Below:
The library opens to a public reading garden.

Drawing:
Site plan

Facing page:
The reading garden creates a buffer between street and library.

077

078

Above left:
The children's reading room is distinguished by its sloping ceiling and curved curtainwall.

Above right:
Soaring peaked roofs create an open atmosphere in the main reading room.

Drawing:
Site plan

079

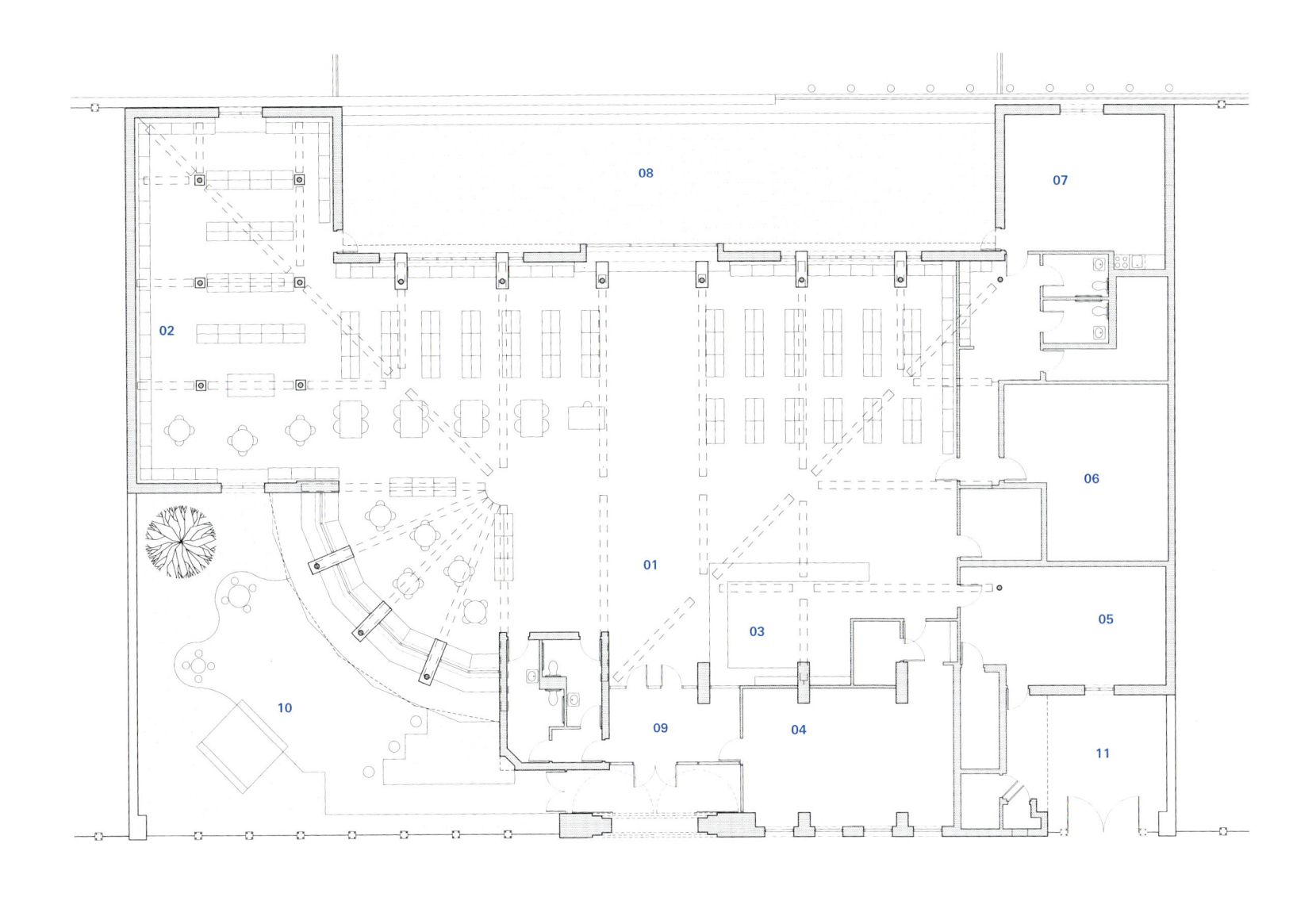

01. Main reading room	02. Children's reading room	03. Circulation desk	04. Meeting room	05. Workroom	06. Mechanical room	07. Staff lounge	08. Open public space
09. Lobby	10. Reading garden	11. Service entrance					

WELCOME
A SCHOOL OF EXCELLENCE
IN PROGRESS

Public Schools

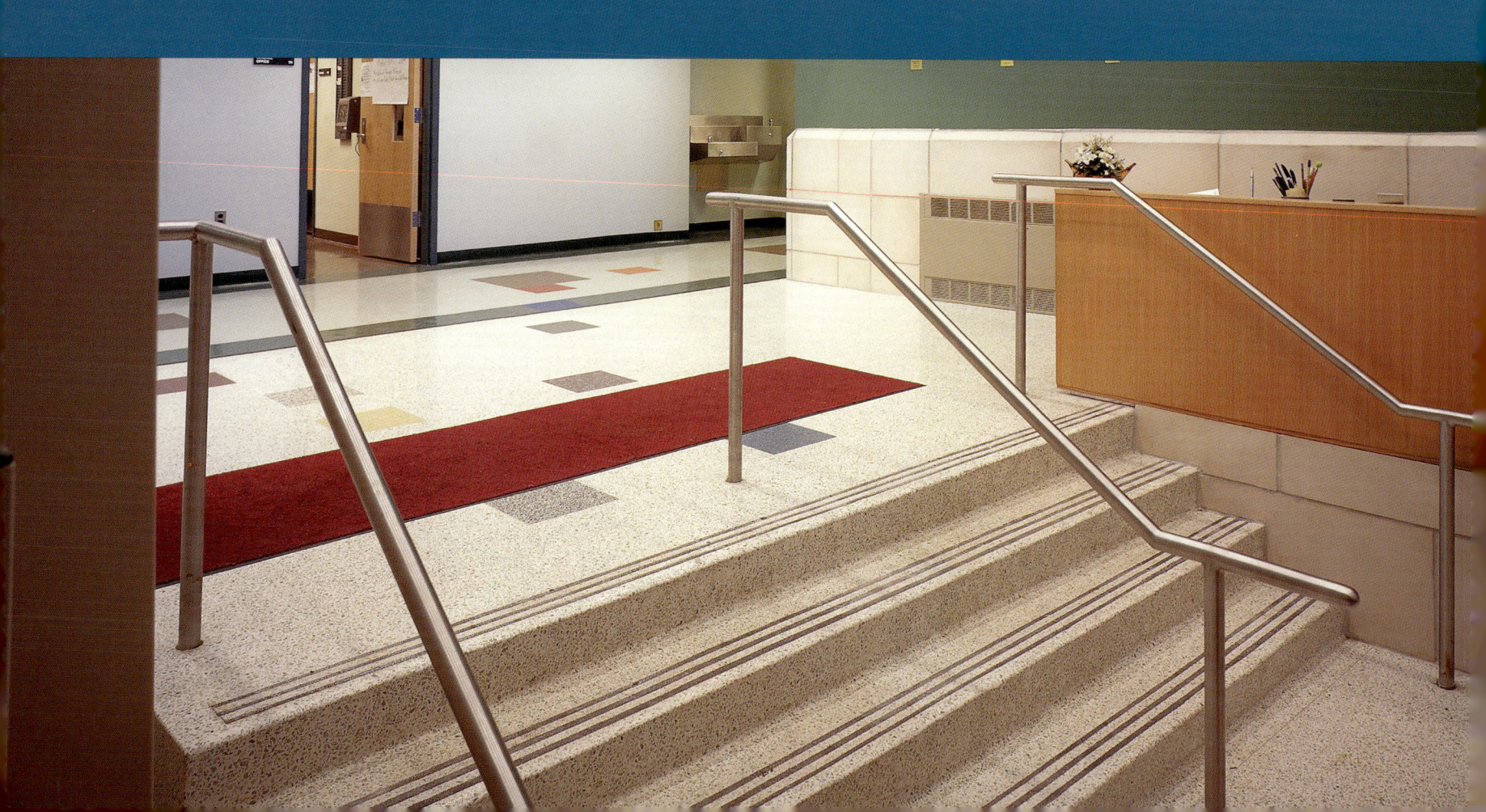

"Grammar school is the child's first introduction to formalized society. It's the first time the child leaves the protection of the home to go into a formalized group environment. You want to design schools so they can function beyond eight-to-three, so even people without children in school can use it and feel that it's a part of their community."

John Ciardullo

I.S. 254
Bronx, New York (1999)

Public schools in the U.S. are in an ideal position to reinstate their public nature. The average American school building is 42 years old, but the average life span for such a building is only 40 years. At the same time, communities are taking a more proprietary view of their schools. Urban schools in particular are undergoing a vitally important review and reduction in size. Schools in which any possibility of community affinity had been denied or overwhelmed by student populations in the mid-thousands are being renovated into several separate, smaller schools. Communities are demanding that new school buildings be designed for populations in the hundreds, and that these new environments be sensitive to the needs of the various age groups, each of which communicates differently among itself and with the community outside of the school.

John Ciardullo Associates' longstanding policy is to embody a social fabric in both programming and architecture. Ciardullo believes that this approach is particularly valuable to public schools because the past 50 years of suburbanization have led us to compartmentalize our community; automatically and artificially we separate both children and the elderly from the rest of the community. The challenge in public school design today is to create a space to appeal to the entire community, despite tightly restricted sites, construction timelines, and budgets. In I.S. 254 Bronx, John Ciardullo Associates used details to create a relatively dramatic and appropriately civic space out of what was an awkward, sloping, L-shaped site.

I.S. 254 is a new school designed for 600 students under the New York City School Construction Authority's Modular Design/Build Program, which limits the modular unit size to a maximum of 14 feet wide, 13 feet four inches high, and 68 feet long. The building also had to be three stories high. The architects counteracted these restrictions architecturally, beginning with the triumph of an entrance experience that is both rewarding and encouraging.

Washington Avenue and East 189th Street bound the site. The primary entrance stands at the midpoint of the building, on Washington Avenue. A generous precast concrete border accentuates the stainless steel doors and implies the school's civic status. Precast concrete is also carried through the interior of the lobby to form a wainscot framing the entry. Above the concrete border is a clerestory window with a decorative stainless steel grate that inspires reverence, rather than dread.

The upward movement created by this exterior detailing is continued on the interior. Two lines of tiles in muted shades direct traffic up three steps into a surprisingly bright two-story lobby. The canted walls and ceiling increase the perceived size of the lobby and foreshorten the distance to the clerestory window and to the vast, open sky beyond. Back lighting from the clerestory window in turn foreshortens the corridors, making them less intimidating. The lobby can be monitored directly from the administrative office across the hall on the first floor and from the second-floor corridor.

In spite of tight restrictions on square footage and building and window heights, the architects responded artfully to the neighboring environment. The brick facing on the first floor and horizontal patterns of expressed brick running in line with the windows on the second and third floors mimic the scale of existing buildings. By carrying the coping around the building, the architects expressed the more exalted nature of a public school. An aluminum clad egress stair, echoing the stainless steel of the primary entrance, leads from the semi-private gymnasium to a semi-public play area chiseled out of the site's eastern side. Plantings hem the area in and soften the yard's concrete surface. A secondary ramped entrance along Washington Avenue, adjacent to the gymnasium, allows people in the community to enter the gym after school hours, making this tightly sited building a resource for the whole community.

083

Drawing:
Front elevation

Above:
A generous precast concrete border accentuates the school's stainless steel doors.

084

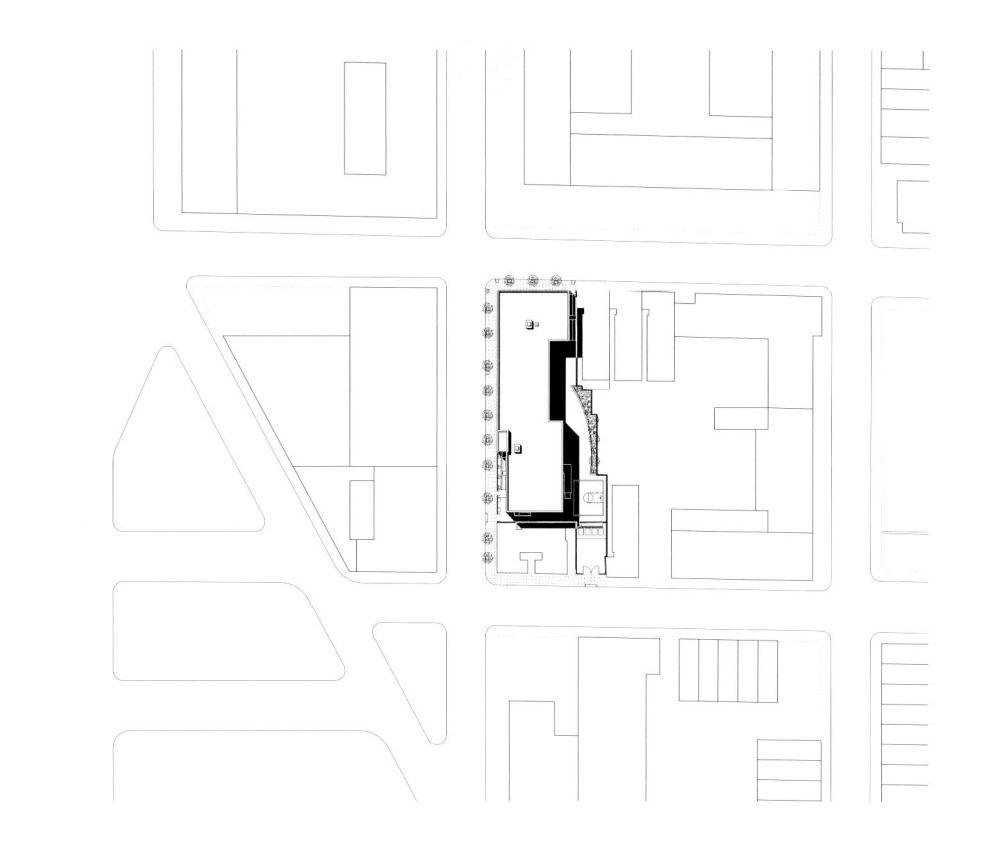

Drawing above:
Site plan

Drawing below:
Rear elevation

Facing page:
The concrete surface
of the rear play area is
softened by plantings.

085

086

Facing page:
The gymnasium is open to the community during off-hours.

Above left:
A clerestory window with a decorative grill sits above the entrance.

Above right:
The entrance can be monitored from the second floor corridor.

088

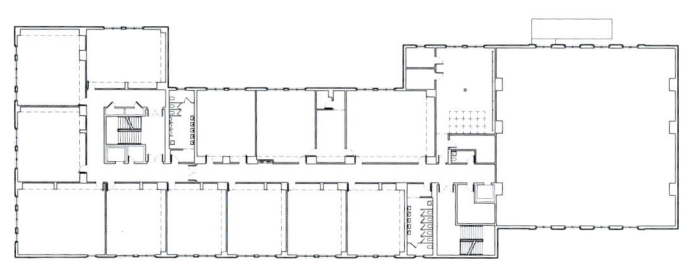

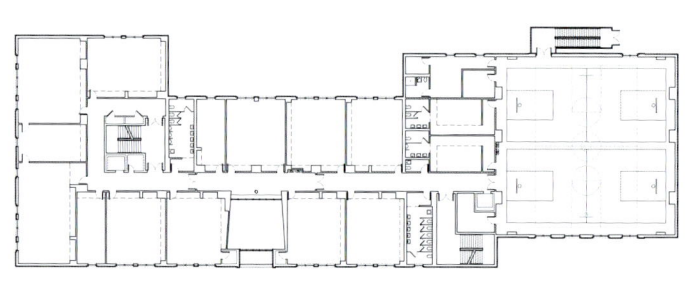

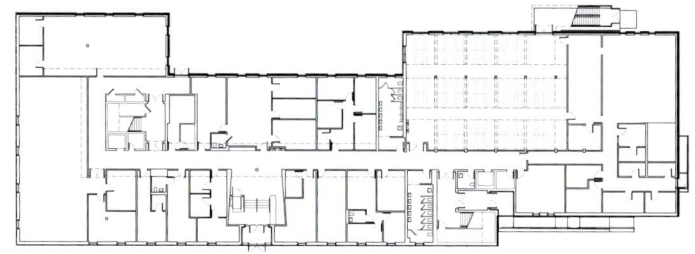

Above:
The aluminum clad stair leads from the gymnasium to the play area.

Drawings bottom to top: First, second, and third floor plans

Facing page: The play area is open to the community.

089

P.S. 242
Queens, New York (2001)

P.S. 242 is an Early Childhood Center at the corner of 137th Street and 31st Road in Queens. John Ciardullo Associates was asked to design from plans prepared by the New York City School Construction Authority. This was relatively difficult because no two sides of the site are parallel. The community's primary mandate was to locate the play area, which doubles as the before-school assembly area, on a residential street, rather than at the rear of the school, as is far too common in urban schools. The architects placed the playground on 31st Road, and a teacher's lounge on the first floor with windows that allow teachers to monitor playing children. The major façade of the building was placed eight feet off of the back property line, through which all servicing is accomplished. The geometry developed from these two placements. While the play area façade is also parallel to the back property line, the architects rotated half of the entry façade 11 1/2 degrees, to a position parallel to 137th Street. The architects then clearly identified this entrance, a slightly recessed corridor between the two non-parallel façades, with a steel channel awning painted bright blue. Because it slices into this irregular face, the entry is dramatic, but also counters any spatial disorientation. A curtainwall entry, running the height of the building, pulls light down the entire length of the corridor.

In contrast to the complexity of the site, P.S. 242, which is designated for pre-kindergarten through third grade, is simply organized, and is defined clearly by fenestration. Functions relating to the whole school are on the first floor: administrative offices, teachers' lounge, guidance office, multipurpose space, lunchroom, and electrical box. On the second floor, punctuated with two pairs of double-hung and two single-hung windows, are four kindergarten classrooms, each averaging 1,000 square feet. Two pairs of double-hung windows define classrooms on the third floor.

The brick banding on the classroom window side is broken abruptly at the blank entry façade that carries the school's numbers, then continues on the other side of the recessed corridor, making a lively public statement. Interior details like bathroom wall tiles, floors, and lunchroom benchs, repeat the bright color scheme initiated outside in the playground and windows.

By responding first to the community's requirements for a nurturing and comfortable outdoor playground, John Ciardullo Associates turned geometric irregularity to advantage and helped to create a lively public school on a difficult site.

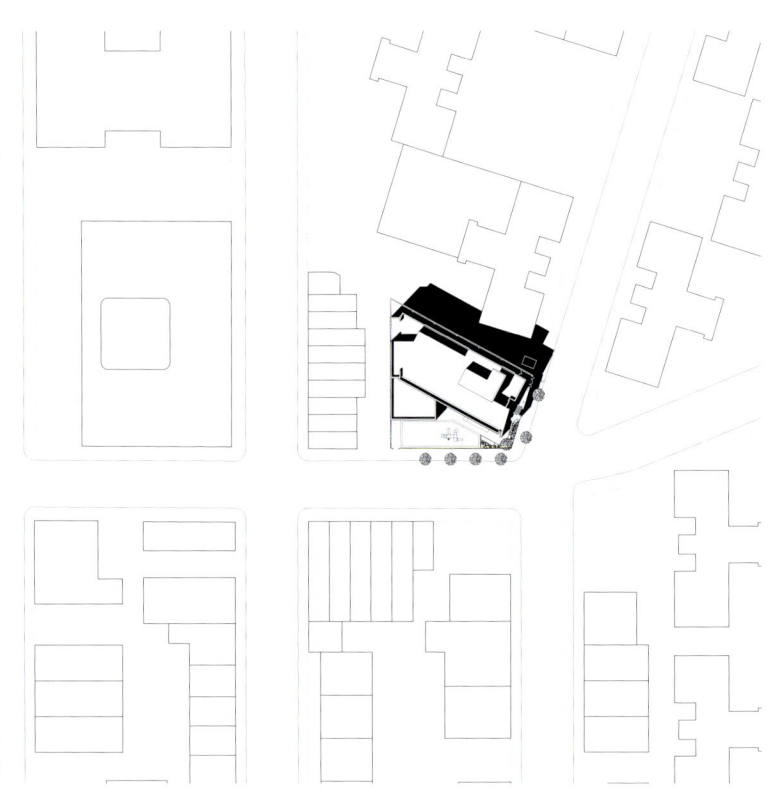

Facing page:
Designing P.S. 242 was a challenge because no two sides of the site are parallel.

Drawing:
Site plan

091

092

Above:
A steel channel awning demarcates the main entrance.

Drawing above:
Second floor plan

Drawing below:
First floor plan

Facing page:
The glass curtain-wall entry, that runs the height of the entire building, fills the interior corridors with light.

093

Above left:
The play area is visible from a teacher's lounge on the first floor.

Above right:
On the façade, single- and double-hung windows demarcate the classrooms.

095

Above:
The community mandated that the play area be located on a residential street.

096

All above:
The bright color scheme initiated in the window frames and awning outside is continued throughout the interior.

Above:
The multipurpose room is located on the first floor.

Edgemont Junior-Senior High School
Scarsdale, New York (2002)

The Edgemont Junior-Senior High School is a comfortably open campus of nine buildings built over the past 50 years that are connected by meandering walks sheltered by concrete breezeways. Like the Edgemont Elementary School, here most of the buildings were built in the 1950s and 1960s. They are one-story structures with flat roofs and aluminum and glass curtainwalls highlighted by primary colored ceramic panels. The campus serves both a general student population and a smaller group of academically gifted Alternative School students, who are more independent than the general students. When the architects received the commission, these students were already established in their own, separate building on the campus, and were discouraged from mingling with the rest of the students by the physical independence of their study space.

The concept of the new facility was to combine a new home for the Alternative School with new science facilities, an art classroom, and five general purpose classrooms. The Alternative School consists of two classrooms, an office, restrooms, and a common space. The science facility consists of chemistry and biology laboratories and a science preparation room.

The design strives to provide separate identities for these functions while providing a singular building on the campus plan. The building reinforces this two-part concept by using two distinct structures and exterior systems for each section. A two-story brick masonry bearing wall and concrete plank floor structure defines the science section and a steel framed brick clad structure defines the Alternative School. Both facilities have a separate exterior entrance while sharing a central two-story internal atrium planned as a common gathering space for all students. The classrooms are organized between a series of three parallel brick masonry walls, which contrast large sections of sloped glazed curtainwalls, providing immediate views of the beautifully landscaped central campus.

The existing library and classroom buildings on either side of the new addition created an irregular spatial relationship. In a gesture that unites the library with other buildings, the architects positioned the Alternative School parallel to the library, and the science facility mass parallel to the existing classroom building. A library, also open to the general public, had to be accessible to the handicapped. John Ciardullo Associates answered this requirement with an elevator tower between the new building and the library, thus allowing direct access to the library by Alternative School students as well.

Without compromising the campus aspect of the High School, these changes emphasize the physical manifestations of both the student and general communities; each new element speaks to the whole, as well as the various parts of the school.

Along with sitework and multiple alterations that allow for public meetings and enlarged stage workroom space, band room, practice room, and music department offices, these additions unify the campus and strengthen the school's presence on the site. The new buildings and additions feature strong brick masonry walls contrasted with large sections of glazed curtainwalls, providing immediate views of the landscaped campus.

This plan for a growing school embraces the already open plan devised in the middle of the century, complementing it with a certain amount of centralized common space. It successfully satisfies the full range of social relationships on the private-public continuum that occur at the highschool level.

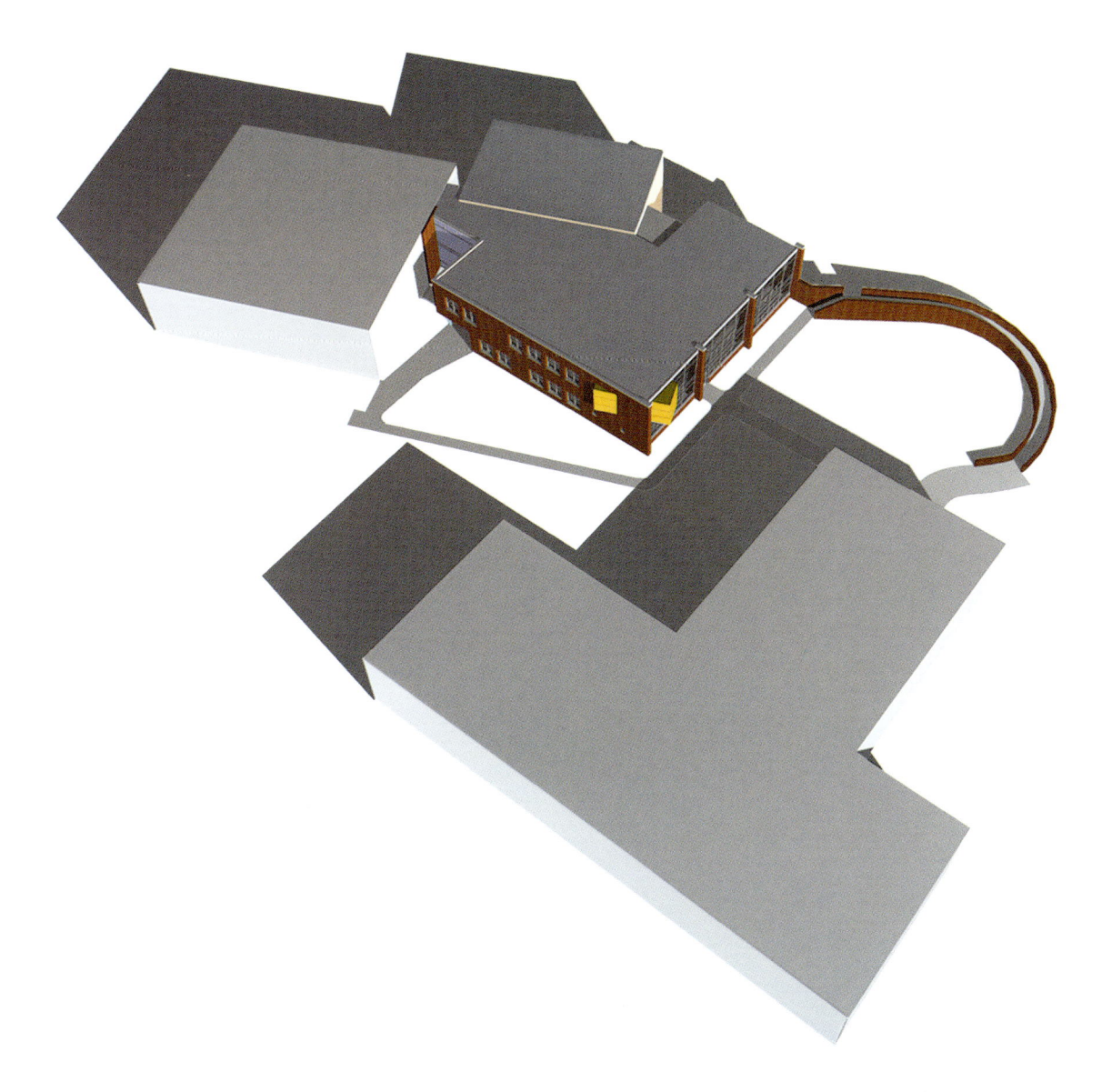

Above:
The two distinct functions of the addition are parallel in plan to the two existing buildings.

099

01.
Classrooms

02.
Science labs

03.
Art room

04.
Storage

05.
Lower level entrance

06.
Upper level enrance

07.
Gifted students classrooms

08.
Office

Drawings left to right:
Lower and upper level plans

Above:
Glazed curtain-walls provide views of the beautifully landscaped campus.

Seely Place Elementary School
Scarsdale, New York (2002)

Seely Place Elementary School, built in several phases during the 1920s and 1930s, is a colonial-style two-story brick building with a distinctive bell tower. Architectural unity had been preserved by additions in the 1940s, 50s, and 60s, but overcrowding threatened the quality of education. To reclaim the semi-public spaces that had been lost to expanding classrooms and storage, John Ciardullo Associates created a semi-circular addition, forming a central axis that extends from the original main entrance. This new path brings students and other members of the community past the intersection with the main corridor, which is double-loaded with classrooms, past the new kindergartens, to the new library, which becomes the central focus of the school.

The 14,000-square-foot addition of steel frame and brick masonry is three stories high. It is sensitive to the original colonial-style architecture and, at the same time, creates modern, functional, open public spaces for the more social activities of the community. The cantilevered brick upper story is dramatically supported by a series of two-story-high Doric columns. Below this is a segmented glazed curtainwall, modern in form and traditional in function, which provides panoramic views of the tree-lined playing fields. An elevator and connecting walkway allow handicap access to the existing lower level, where the cafeteria is located. The cafeteria, enclosed by a two-story glazed curtainwall from the library above, also acts as a multipurpose room, serving both the school and the community. A science lab and conference room are included, along with three standard and three special education classrooms. Fittingly, the community spaces–library, lunchroom, and multi-purpose area–become the effective focus of the school.

The architects also reconfigured 8,500 square feet to create spaces for a band room, instrument storage area, faculty room, and school psychologist's office. Site work upgraded the parking areas and some athletic fields, changed circulation patterns to create new drop off areas for improved student safety, and incorporated new paved areas for additional parking. The minimal budget, the greatest portion of which was used on construction costs, was far below that normally spent by school districts. John Ciardullo Associates encouraged the client to boldly imagine the most effectual reconfigurations, and then worked with the existing buildings and landscape to design the most cost-effective additions, taking into consideration the community's social and architectural contexts.

103

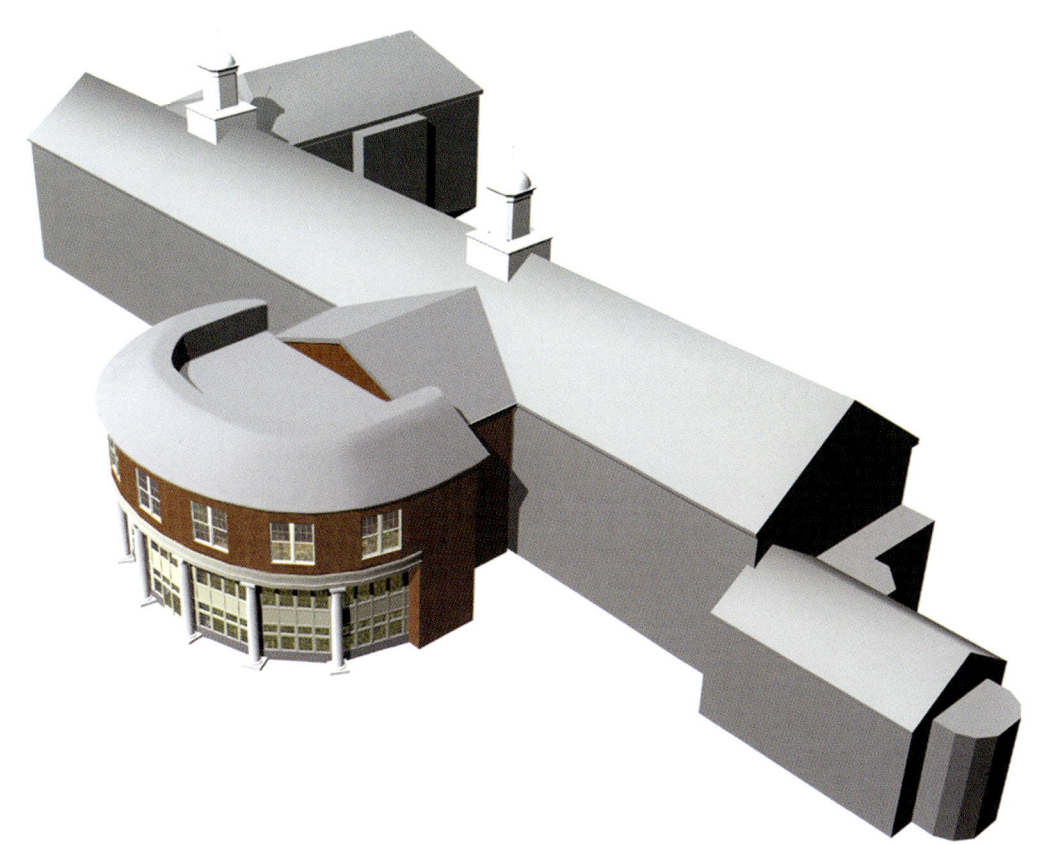

Above:
Rear elevation

Below:
The addition is sensitive to the existing colonial-style architecture.

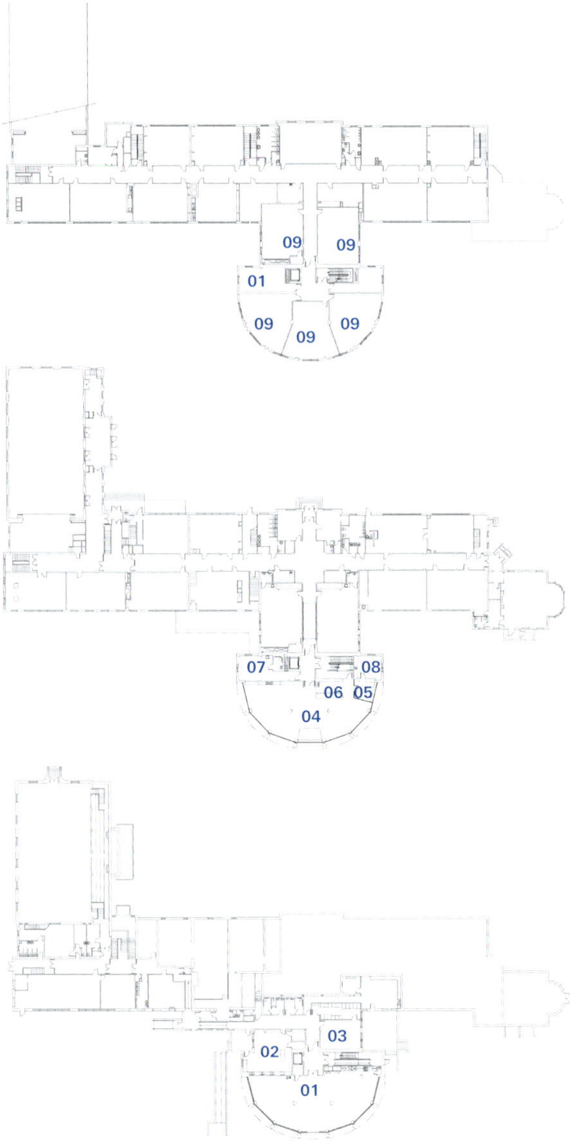

| 01. Lunch room | 02. Science lab | 03. Band room | 04. Library | 05. Office | 06. Circulation desk | 07. Office | 08. Book storage |

| 09. Classrooms | 10. Nurse office | Drawing left: Side elevation | Drawings right bottom to top: Basement, first, and second floor plans | | | | Facing page: Two-story-high Doric columns dramatically support the addition's brick upper story. |

105

Greenville Elementary School
Scarsdale, New York (2002)

The Greenville Elementary School is a one-story trident-shaped structure built in two phases during the 1950s and 1960s. Before John Ciardullo Associates reconsidered the school's architecture in terms of the social facts of school life, the three fingers of the existing trident stretched out toward the playing fields, one of them terminating in a gymnasium. This arrangement was frustrating in its disassociation. Each finger was an independent wing allocated to two grades and allowed no intermingling of students–no community–except through chance encounters in the distant connecting corridors at the trident's base. The architects completed the circulation, adding a connecting semi-public space to the end of each wing, which can also be used by the community at large. The connecting corridors are steel and glass. They offer views of the interior courtyards, which were created between the wings by the addition, or out onto the playing fields. The new library, multipurpose room (with stage and storage facilities), and science library can each function independently from one another and from the existing classrooms, effectively transforming the school into a community center whenever necessary.

The school stands on top of a hill. The new community spaces face south. The exposure is blocked by steel projections jutting out from the glass curtainwall, finished in bright yellow. Along with the materials palette of the addition, this coloration maintains the aesthetics of the original building. Although the wings face the playing fields, the circular form of the library that caps the central wing redirects attention back to the school's interior, minimizing the intrusive effect.

John Ciardullo Associates also proposed alterations to create two classrooms, a faculty room, special education rooms, a testing room, and restrooms. The existing multipurpose room was modified into a two-level lunchroom.

In response to the need for community space, the architects connected the larger public spaces and equipped them with separate heating systems, allowing any or all of these spaces to be secured for after-school and weekend use by the community. The new multipurpose room can be used as a gymnasium as well as an auditorium, seating over 500 people for both school and community functions. Just as in Seely Place Elementary, in Greenville Elementary, the library, open for everyone's education, is at the building's core, architecturally stating the importance of the school to the community.

Above:
The additions create gathering spaces within the otherwise dispersed school.

108

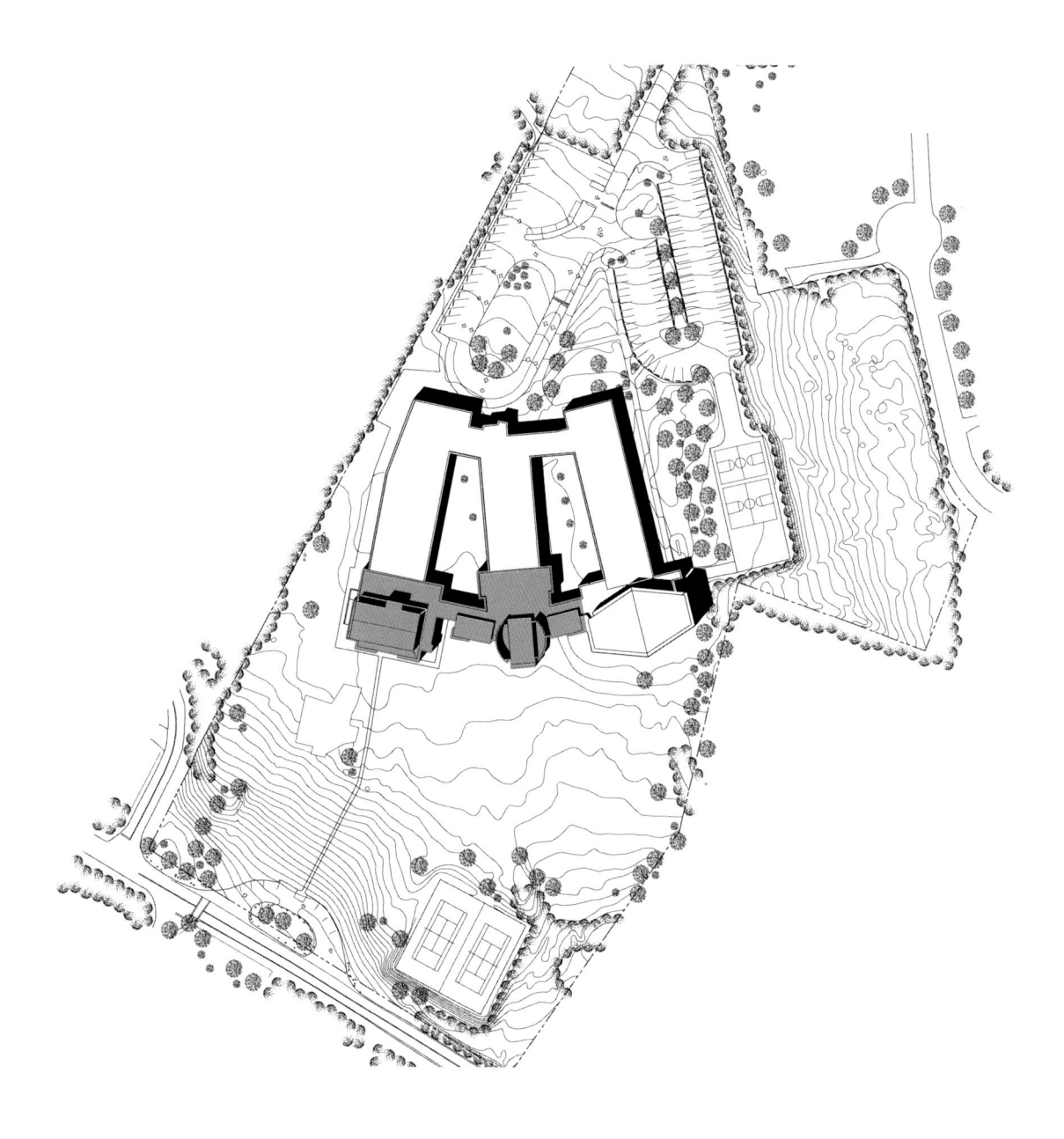

Drawing:
Site plan

Above:
The materials palette and coloration of the addition maintains that of the existing structure.

110

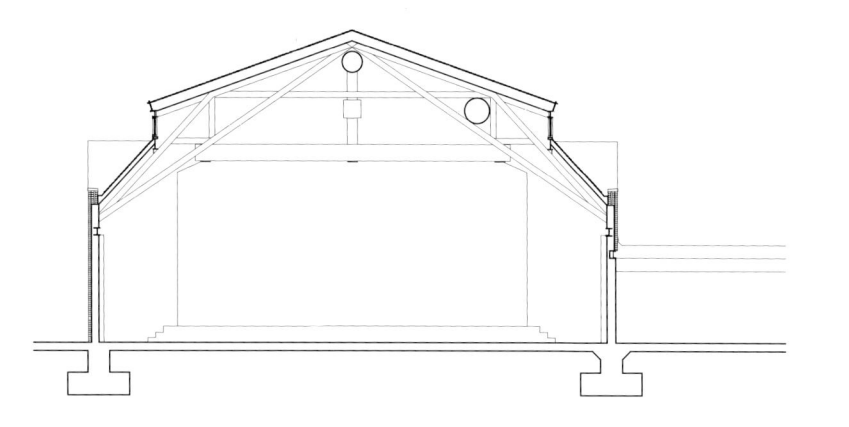

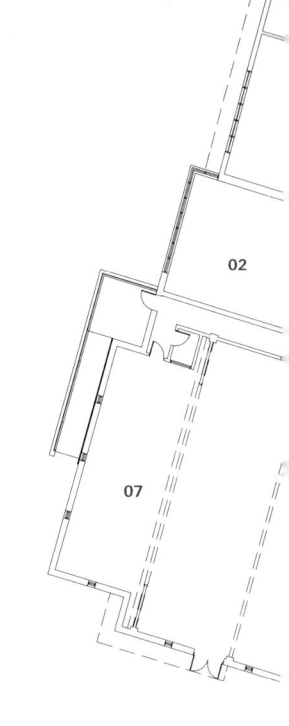

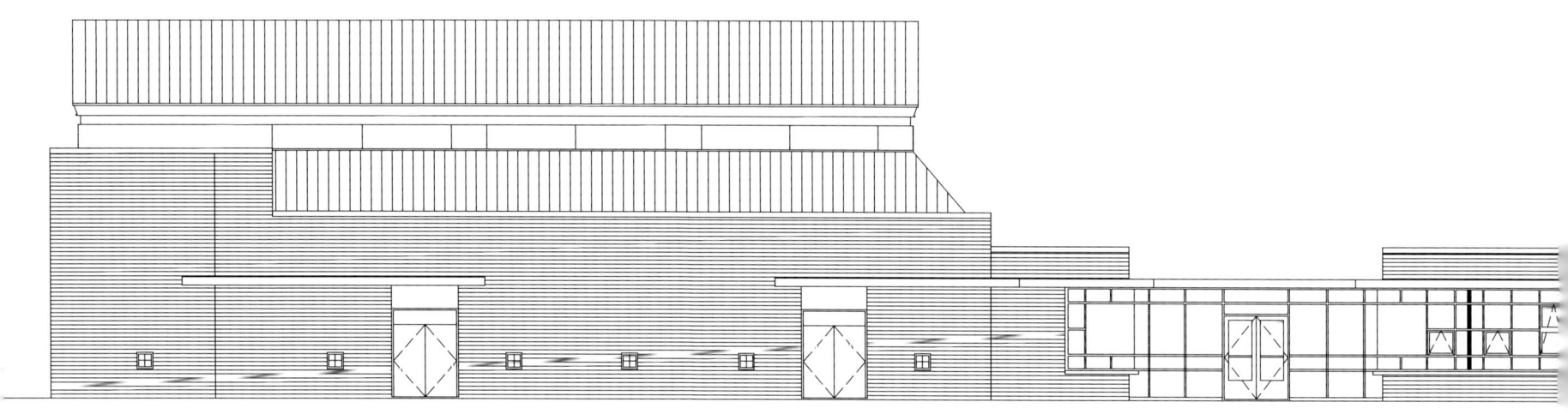

Across page:
Rear elevation

Above:
Section multipurpose space

01.
Multipurpose space

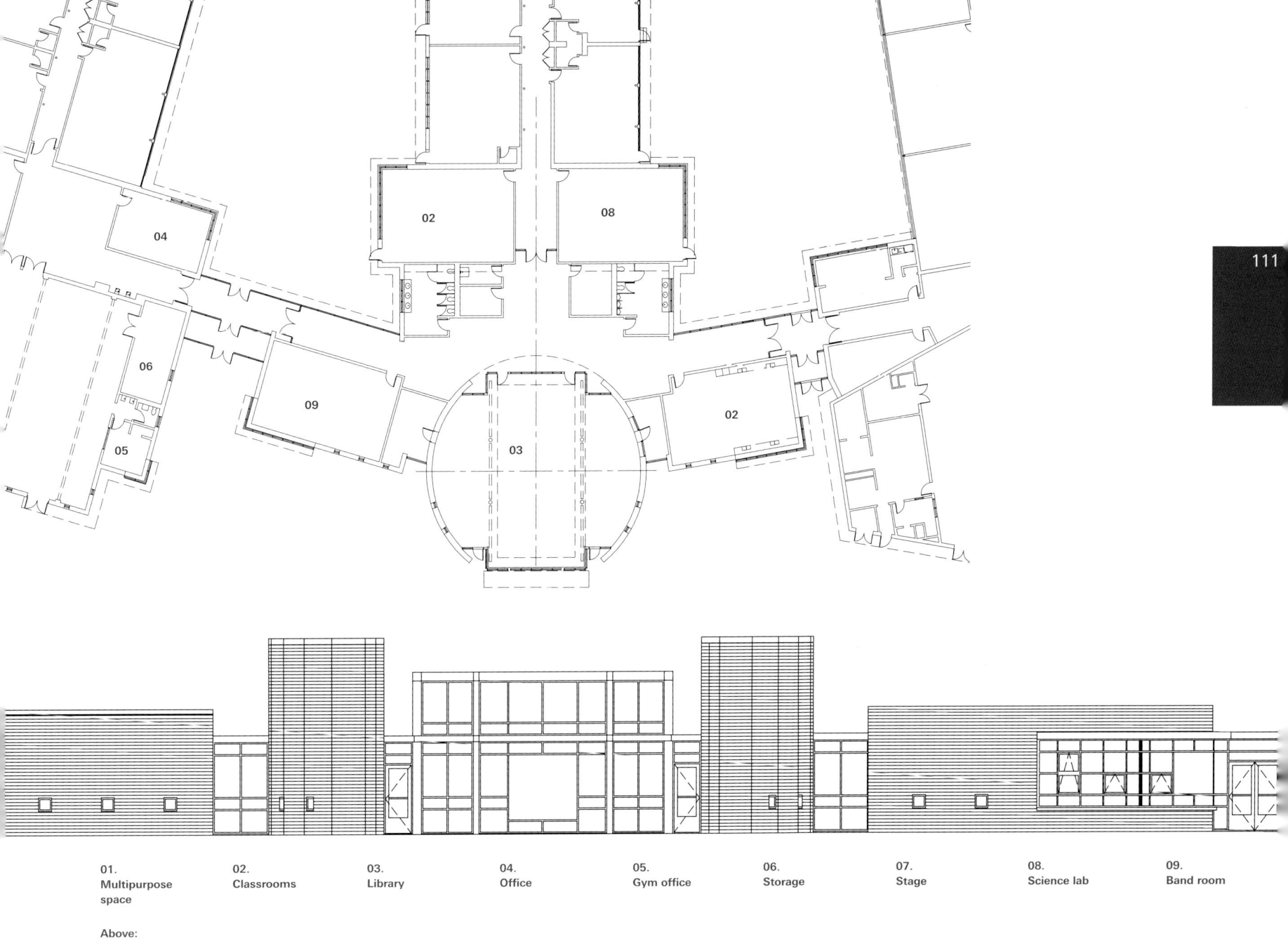

02.
Classrooms

03.
Library

04.
Office

05.
Gym office

06.
Storage

07.
Stage

08.
Science lab

09.
Band room

Above:
Plan

P.S. 268
Queens, New York (2002)

Public School 268 Queens is a new primary school with a separate mandate to accommodate a city-wide program for physically and mentally challenged children in grades K through five, as well as the main stream student body. Three distinct environments bound the site, which originally held a large, odd-shaped catering hall. Jamaica Avenue, the northern boundary, is a bustling commercial/light industrial street; 175th and 176th Streets are residential; and the southeast boundary abuts the side yards of private houses.

The community's requirements were difficult to fulfill on this tight site: a 94,000-square-foot school, a play area removed from Jamaica Avenue, separate entrances for elementary and pre-K students, a semi-public assembly area that is fully visible from the administration office, and several spaces open to the public outside of school hours. Therefore, a good number of the basic design decisions were direct responses to the community's needs and the restrictions of the site.

The exterior elevations respond directly to the school's interior organization. They engage the community by respecting its residential scale. The fenestration and playful details indicate the variety of activity inside the school, and relate visually to the general tone of nearby buildings.

Because it was ruled out as an entrance or play area, the busy Jamaica Avenue boundary, which faces north, was chosen as the classroom side. The neutral façade on Jamaica Avenue, with rows of double-hung windows on three stories, indicates the classrooms and corresponds with other buildings on the commercial street. The dark gray band of brick on the first floor indicates the distinct educational area set aside for city-wide preschool students. Four very large pre-K classroom windows feature bright yellow frames that attract public attention at the corner of 176th Street and Jamaica Avenue; the classroom becomes the venue of a lively street event. On 175th Street the outdoor play area serves as a transition from the residential streetscape.

Before classes, students may easily queue up in the play yard, or, in inclement weather, go into the adjacent cafeteria, which doubles as a community room. To reach the auditorium, the students climb a convenient staircase to the intersection of the two main corridors on the second floor. The community demanded that the entry and all stair tower egresses be located away from Jamaica Avenue. The bright red stair tower structures shoot up the sides of the building on 175th and 176th Streets, bringing natural light into the double-loaded classroom corridors.

The challenge to allow free play on such a restricted site yielded several thoughtful solutions. The original request for outdoor play space facing 175th Street predicated a community access core where other semi-public spaces would be stacked. The architects arranged these spaces as follows: the lobby and cafeteria on the first floor, the auditorium on the second floor, the library and dance studio on the third floor, the gym on the fourth floor, and the rooftop play area. A bright yellow, two-story curtainwall articulates these spaces. The secure rooftop play area is sheltered by a detailed steel structure articulated by double columns and painted sky blue, recalling a trellis or arbor, as opposed to the prison yard model many rooftop playgrounds seem to follow. On this extremely tight site, John Ciardullo Associates created a single building that supports a plethora of educational and social functions, without sacrificing efficiency. This was achieved by allowing the form to closely follow the function, and opening the door to the possibilities inherent in the constraints.

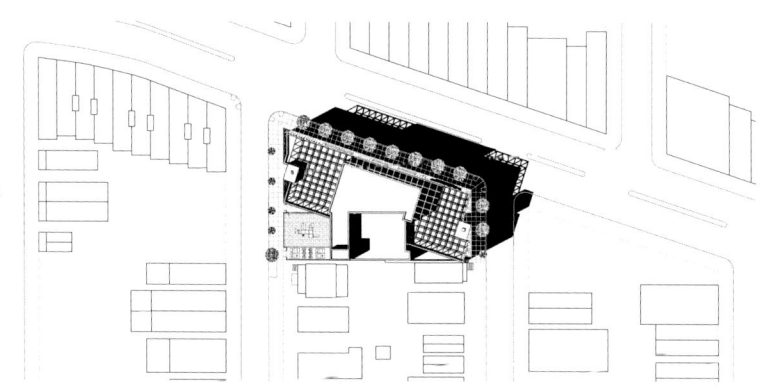

Facing page:
The entrance and play area were located on 175th street, away from busy Jamaica Avenue.

Drawing:
Site plan

113

114

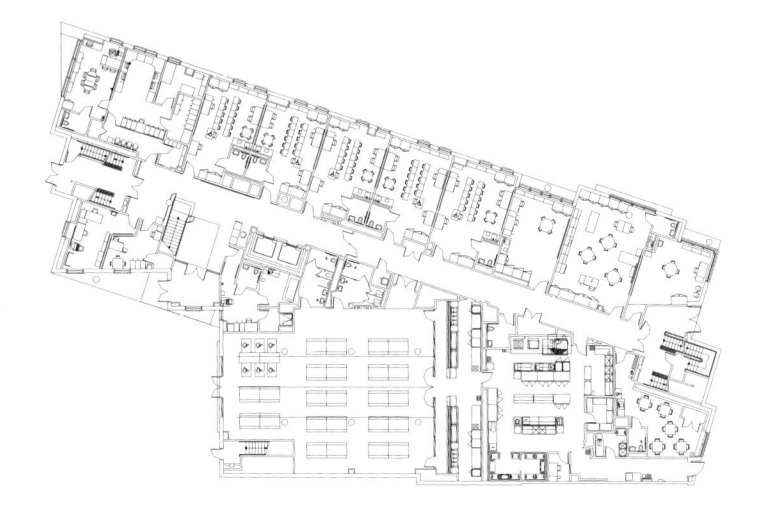

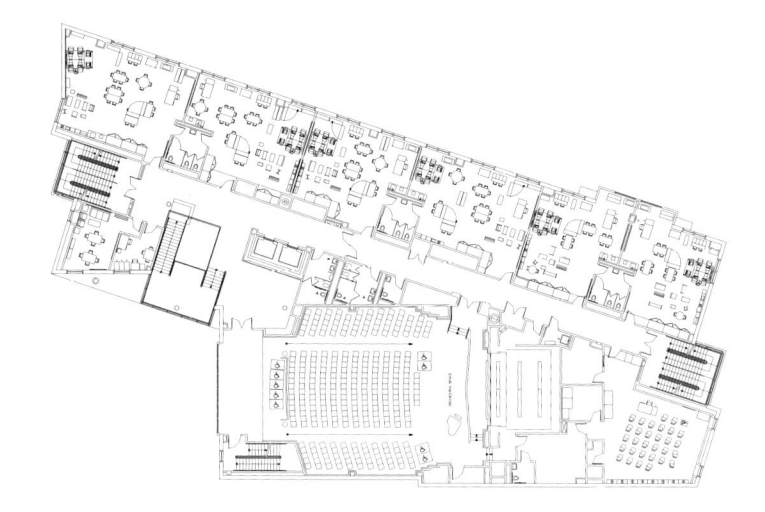

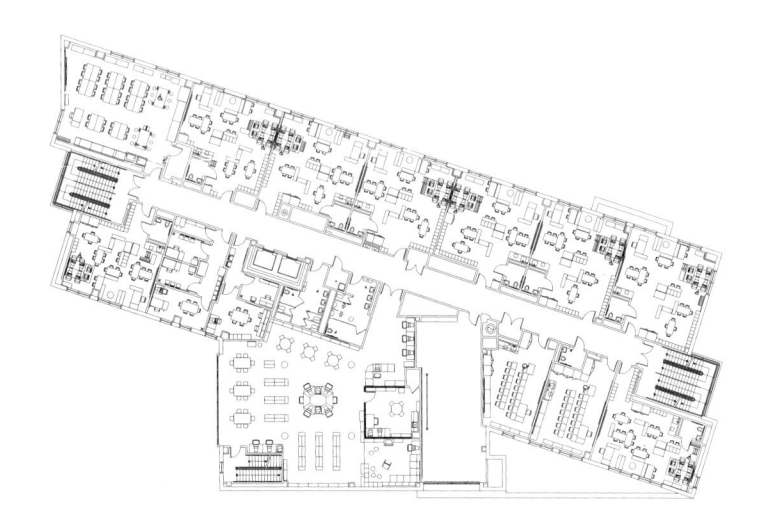

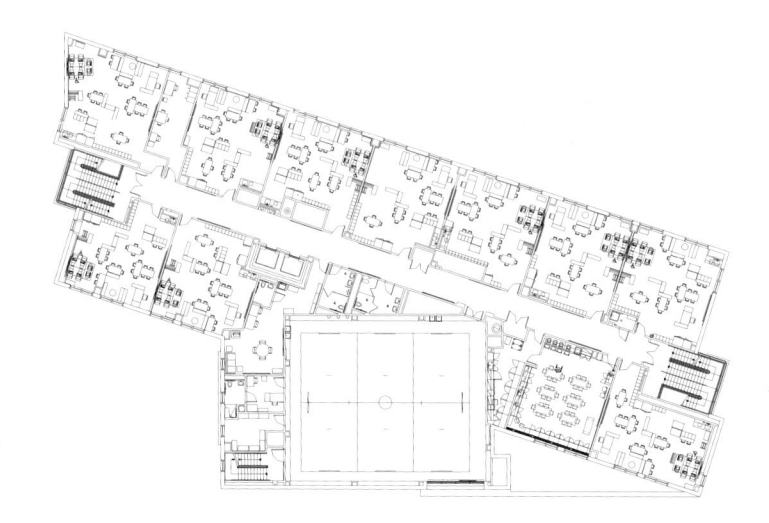

Above left:
First floor

Above right:
Second floor

Below left:
Third floor

Below right:
Fourth floor

Facing page:
The neutral façade on Jamaica Avenue relates to other buildings on the commercial street.

115

P.S. 166
Queens, New York (2002)

P.S. 166 was built in the 1930s. By 1999, when John Ciardullo Associates received the commission for a 45,000-square-foot addition from the NYC School Construction Authority, the school had exceeded its original capacity due to a growing student population. The four-story school, which occupied 95 percent of its site, needed to accommodate an additional 350 students and a cafeteria/multipurpose space large enough for all. The only space available for the addition was the postage stamp-sized playground, which stood next to a two-story, brick, multi-family dwelling, representative of the predominate architecture in the neighborhood. To minimize any disruption and take advantage of the school's established status, the architects sought first to create a visual transition between the massive existing school and the smaller neighboring buildings, one that would be sympathetic to the streetscape already familiar to the community. This was achieved by breaking the span of the new façade in half with masing that reflects the elevations of the neighboring buildings. Voids in the façade represent residential driveways. The connection between the existing school and the addition is recessed slightly, as is the mid-way point in the addition.

The material palette of the addition, which includes precast limestone façade and brick infill, matches the existing building and reduces the intrusive effect of a new building placed in an old neighborhood. The medallion motif is the architects' interpretation of a 1930s vernacular style. Interior walls finished with tiles of contrasting colors, which are illustrated with numbers and letters, also follow this interpretation. In the cafeteria and servery, the unifying 30s-era material element is stainless steel. Stainless soffits in the vaulted cafeteria ceiling and brushed stainless lighting fixtures express the streamlined style familiar from the past.

In the school's original organization, the administrative suite was inconveniently located on the second floor. For this space, the architects claimed the former multipurpose room on the first floor, which faces 35th Avenue, thus consolidating all functions relating to the whole school–all the semi-public spaces–on the first floor. Through the egress link off of 33rd Street, service vehicles and community members can easily access the addition, which, due to a separate air conditioning and heating system, can function independently after school hours, opening this public school to the public.

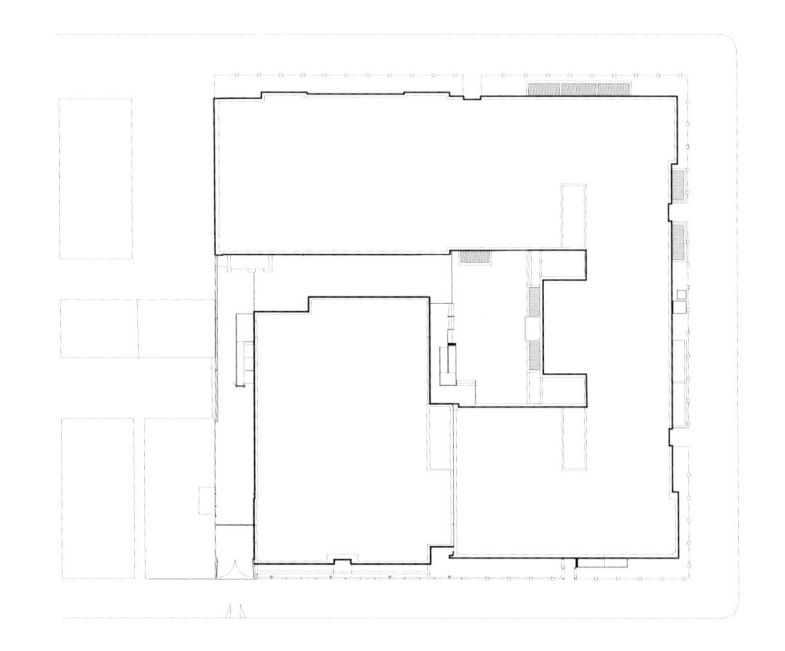

Facing page:
The only space for the addition was a small playground beside a residential building.

Drawing:
Site plan

117

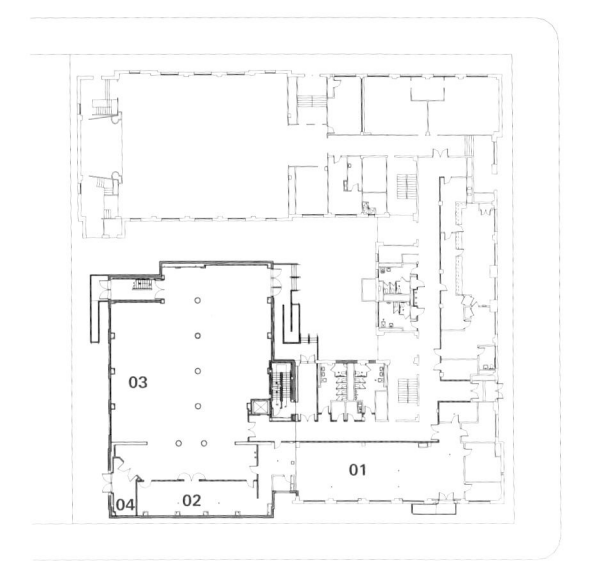

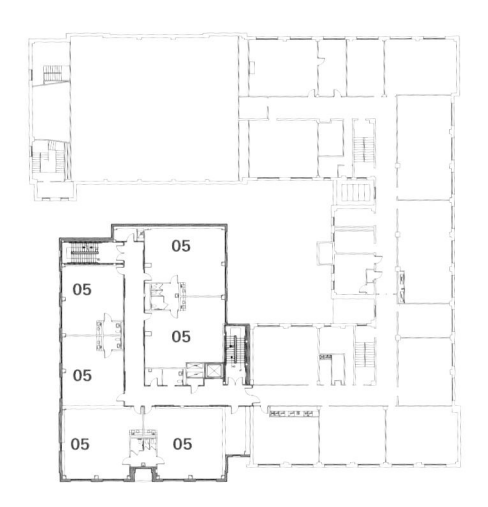

01.
Kitchen

02.
Servery

03.
Cafeteria/
multipurpose space

04.
Cafeteria entrance

05.
Classrooms

Above left:
First floor

Above right:
Second floor

Below:
Elevation

Facing page:
By breaking the façade into massings that reflect the neighboring buildings, sensitivity to context was achieved.

119

120

All above:
Stainless steel in the servery and cafeteria, as well as tile walls, relate to the 30s vernacular of the existing building.

121

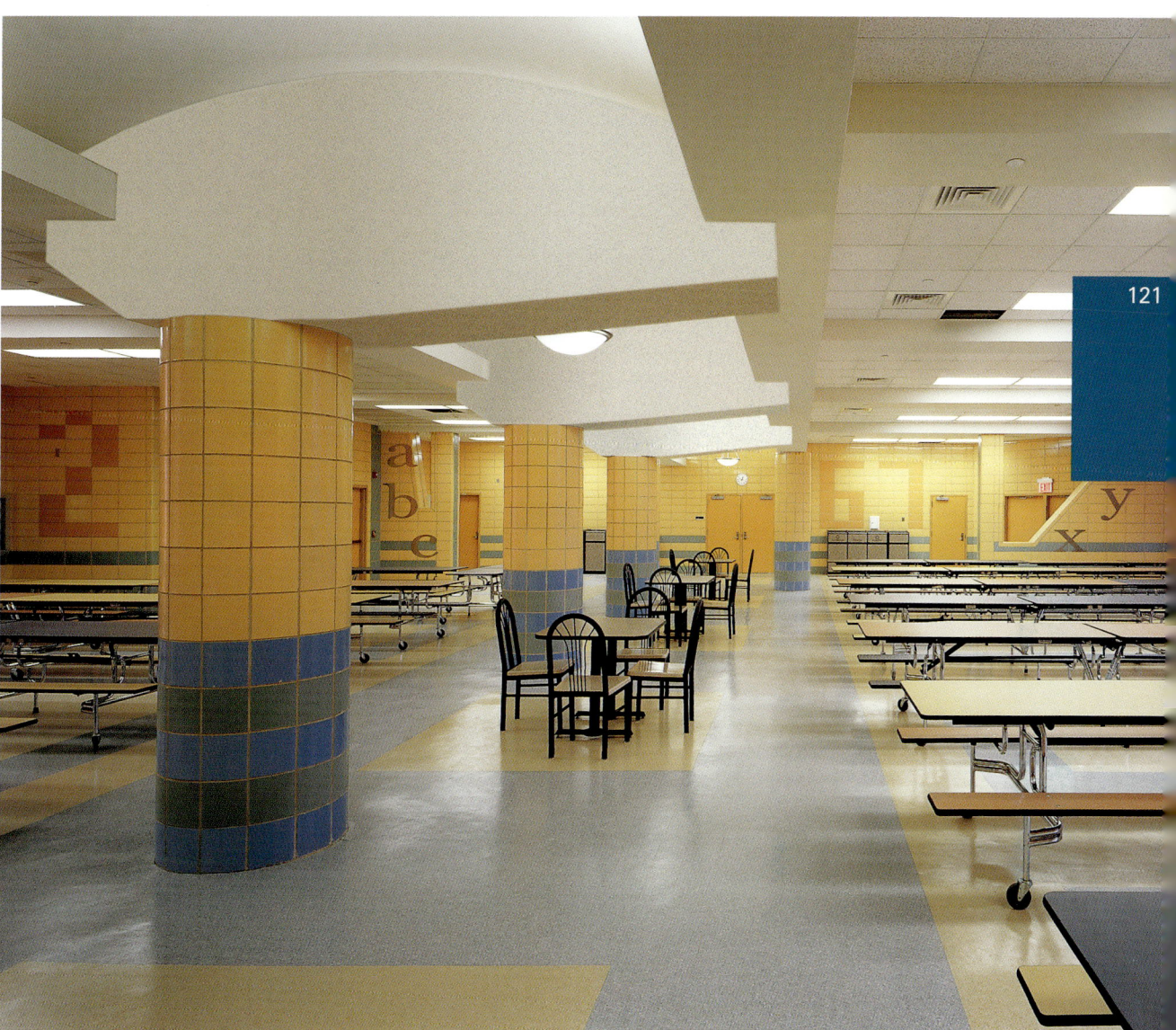

122 Multi-family Housing

" These are not glory jobs; we took projects that architects would never think of as design projects and made them design projects. No one had done low-rise in the government sector. We were the first, and we set a standard. I wanted to show that you can give people quality, a lot more than what they had been given. You can create raised courtyards and private outdoor spaces; you can create communal space, which everybody shares. Some units can have private entries. Some can have entrances on the street and entrances on the courtyard. It's safe. The people who live in our multi-family housing structures have taken pride, and they've put themselves into their environment. The fact is, these places have become their homes."

John Ciardullo

Plaza Borinquen
Bronx, New York (1975)

Plaza Borinquen is a low-scale, scatter site development in the Mott Haven section of the Bronx. At the time it was built, vandalism and decay plagued the city's 1960s-era "superblock" high-rise multi-family housing projects, and many of the site's surrounding buildings were scorched shells. Little hope graced the outlook of the Federal Housing Authority. Rather than simply aiming for a physical or formal solution to a housing problem, John Ciardullo Associates designed each element of Plaza Borinquen with the conviction that the new tenants could live a satisfying life there. The development became a new prototype for public housing.

John Ciardullo had conceived of Plaza Borinquen in his third year of graduate school at Harvard University. It was constructed in 1975 as part of an infill housing program, in which people are moved from substandard to new housing that is erected on vacant lots in their own neighborhoods. This practice physically renews the neighborhood without interfering with established social structures. The architectural decisions John Ciardullo Associates made on Plaza Borinquen also took that existing social structure equally seriously. The project proved beyond a doubt that, if all aspects of the private/public continuum are addressed, even in low-income urban housing people can be comfortable and in control of the spaces where their lives unfold. Plaza Borinquen is an environment where inner city residents can enjoy privacy within their homes and the free use of semi-public open spaces, while identifying with consecutively larger groups beyond the family, including those outside the community boundary.

Plaza Borinquen occupies several sites in the area between 138th and 140th Streets, and Willis and Brooke Avenues. It reestablishes a cohesive neighborhood by approximating the existing structures in scale and density. The architects organized the site to echo the distinct social units on the private-public continuum, beginning with the basic unit of the family. When two or more of these units are combined, the most basic of communities is established–a multi-family unit. The conventional, low-income, tower-like developments of the era had completely erased semi-public spaces where families could interact. These behemoths replaced such spaces with public areas that were too big, too open, and too impersonal to foster neighborhood intimacy or allow more than a few lower-floor residents to watch their children play outside. Ciardullo convinced the Federal Housing Authority that rear-yard entries, open to the public via two paths, would not invite strangers to enter the space, but, on the contrary, would encourage residents to claim the area as their own, thus fostering an awareness of community security. And while the architects achieved the necessary density, 45 units per acre, the external architecture of the units is consciously modeled after townhouses. Courtyards and front porch stoops to make residents conscious of their own spaces, and of their identity within the created community.

Multi-family housing projects do not lend themselves to the creation of privacy. Particularly in higher density housing, the strangers in our midst, even directly on our property lines, threaten to intrude psychologically and physically upon the community of residents. However, through its site layout, floor plans, exterior detailing, and landscaping, Plaza Borinquen repeatedly enforces a neighborhood-scale hierarchy of space. The FHA 236 housing program, under which Plaza Borinquen was built, determined small square-foot limitations, which John Ciardullo Associates interpreted with sensitivity to the private-public continuum. Inside, the architects buffered more private areas, such as bedrooms and baths, from the more public living area, dining area, and kitchen, often locating them on different levels. Most of the 88 units feature three- and four-bedroom interlocking triplex apartments. Unlike the double-loaded corridors with single entrances used in nearby low-rise housing developments, the lower- and upper-entrances that separate units in Plaza Borinquen support family identities. Thanks to the interlocking arrangement, all the units' kitchens have windows looking out onto the semi-public space, each three-story unit has its own garden entrance from either the courtyard or the street side, and every resident can see both the street and courtyard sides of the Plaza's outdoor space.

Facing page:
The interior courtyard is divided between a semi-public area and semi-private raised areas.

125

It was in his early years, when he designed this prototypical housing, that Ciardullo formed his policy centering on the private-public continuum. The firm's work is still anchored by concepts forged then: pride of ownership, the necessity of absolute privacy, and public intercourse that every human being craves. In multi-family housing, these simple solutions transform "housing" into "homes." More than a quarter century after the construction of Plaza Borinquen, tenants still enclose, landscape, and decorate their private outdoor spaces with individuality and pride.

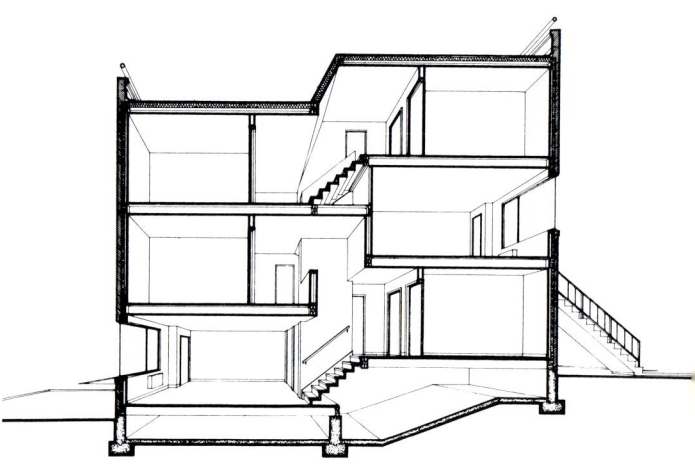

Above left:
A stair leads up from the living, dining, and kitchen spaces of this triplex to the bed and bathrooms.

Drawing:
Section of triplex units

Above:
The living area is
on a separate floor
from the bedrooms
of this two-bedroom
duplex.

128

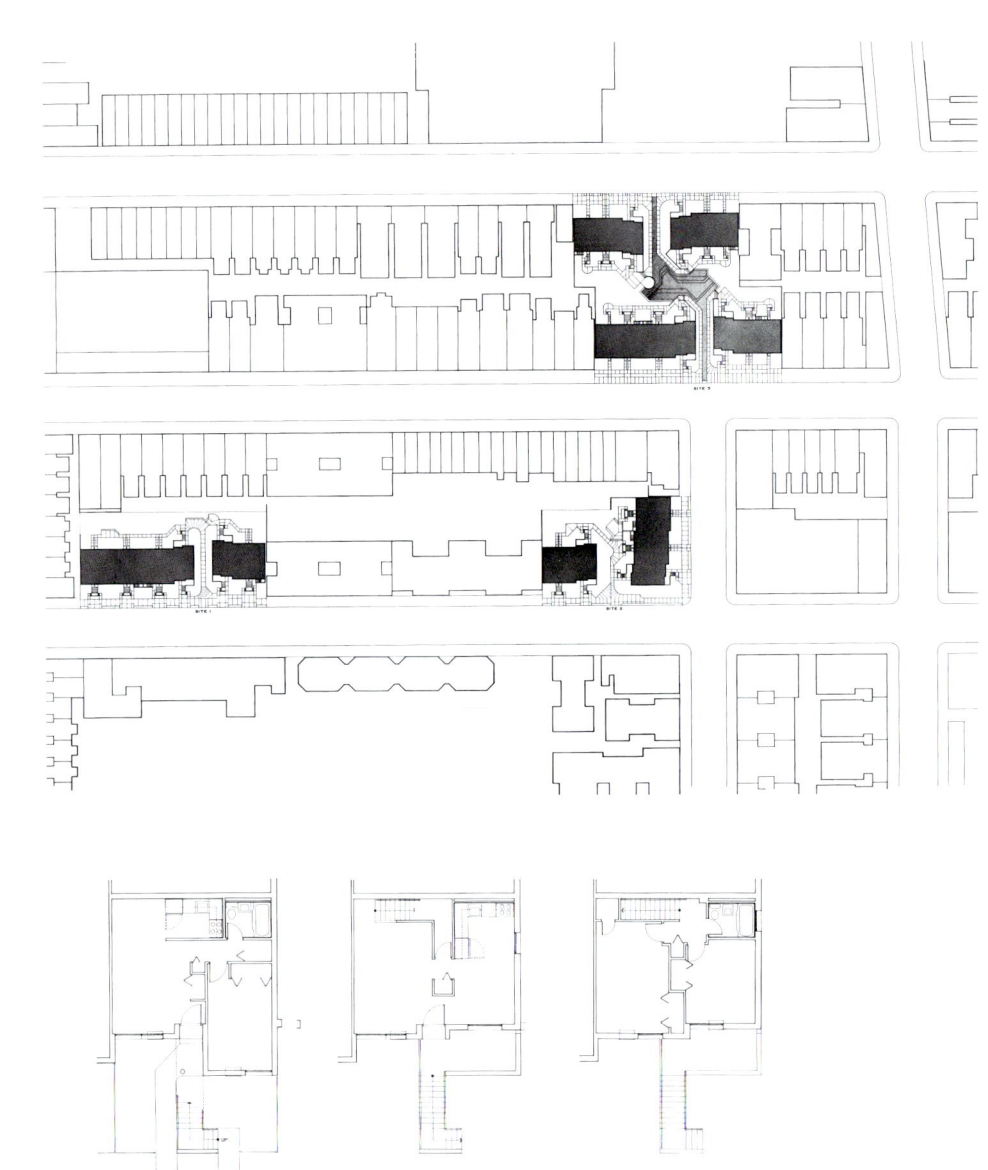

Drawing above:
Site plan

Drawings below:
Floor plans of one- and two-bedroom units

Above:
Private rear yard entries encourage residents to claim the space as their own.

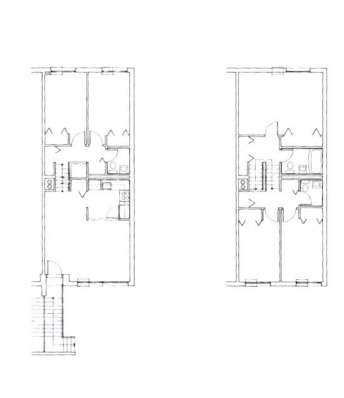

Above:
The buildings were consciously modeled on townhouses.

Drawings left:
Floor plans for three-bedroom units.

Drawings right:
Floor plans for four-bedroom units.

130

Facing page:
The semi-public courtyard is free for the use of all of the plaza's residents

Above:
Wide open paths lead from the street to the courtyard.

Maria Lopez Plaza
Bronx, New York (1982)

John Ciardullo had the urban family in mind when designing Maria Lopez Plaza, a 216-unit project in the Melrose section of the Bronx. Every design decision encourages families to recognize and reap the opportunities for privacy, leisure, safety, and true community within the city. The mid-rise structure, in the traditional inner-courtyard layout, is seven stories high, but its organization, which reflects the needs and desires of families, reminds residents of single-family dwellings in a neighborhood. The client, the South Bronx Community Housing Corporation, asked John Ciardullo Associates to create housing where residents would take active maintenance and security roles. The architects interpreted this as a mandate to give each family or individual the rights to private and community space, which, if genuine, naturally imply responsibility towards those spaces.

To make the structure smaller in scale and help families keep track of their members and their neighbors, the architects built the dense housing portions, two six-story and two seven-story wings, at the perimeter of the city block, thus creating a private tenants' courtyard. The larger, family-oriented duplex units are at the base of the seven-story wings so children can play in secluded safety, monitored by parents and other adults from the courtyard, the private gardens of the ground-floor duplex units, the semi-enclosed exterior corridors, or the nearby apartments. The semi-public courtyard is accessed through two opposing corner stair towers and can be seen from semi-enclosed balconies on the third and fifth floors. These balconies serve as entrances to the upper level duplexes.

In the seven-story wings, simplex units arranged along an interior corridor are located above the second floor. The third through sixth floors of the two wings are composed of duplex units, accessed from the open galleries and open external stairs on the courtyard side. From the outside, the horizontal galleries and vertical stairs visually outline the free movement of residents from public to private spaces.

Although there are no fences on the property, the building itself bars the entry of strangers. On the street sides, individual concrete walkways perpendicular to the public sidewalk effectively define private front yards. These are echoed in the semi-private backyards abutting the interior courtyard garden.

The private exterior entrances of the first floor apartments establish visual continuity with the surrounding neighborhood, and, for the residents, reinforce the physical truth of the building. Although it is a high-density housing project, with 75-80 units per acre, the organization of the entire site gives residents as much outside space as would a private residence.

Anyone living in, visiting, or passing by Maria Lopez Plaza is not confronted by an impersonal block of brick. To enter the complex is to experience a rich transition from public, to semi-public, to semi-private, and finally to private space. The public sidewalk expands to lead residents into the building through a subtracted corner. The entrance has a security area, stairs down to a community room, and a passage to the interior courtyard. Above, there are laundry rooms enclosed by glass, so that people feel connected to the street, observing the comings and goings of their neighbors while they do their laundry. Nearly 20 years after construction, the building and grounds of Maria Lopez Plaza remain in excellent condition, proving that tenants have taken great pride in their homes while building a strong community.

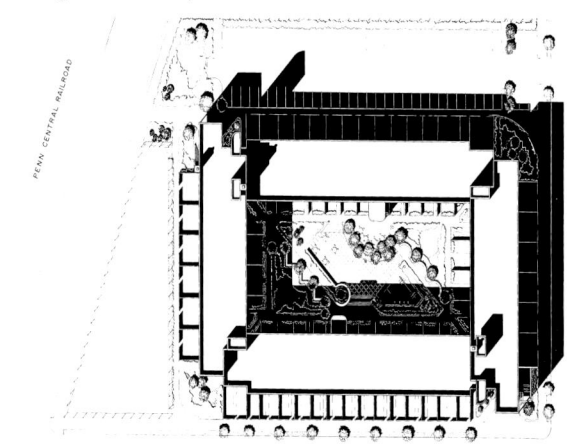

Facing page:
Two six-story and two seven-story wings, arranged at the perimeter of the block, create a private tenants' courtyard.

Drawing:
Site plan

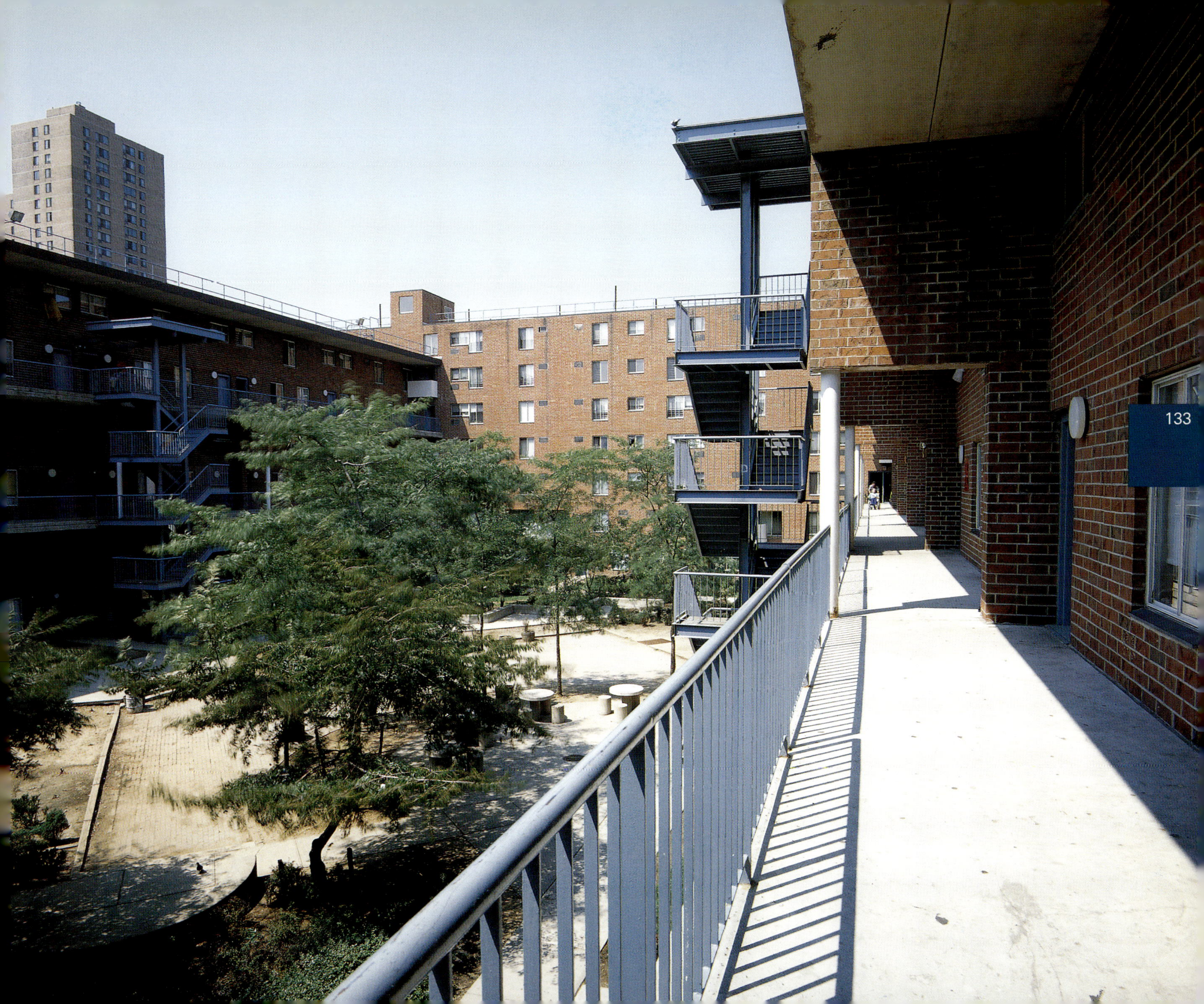
133

134

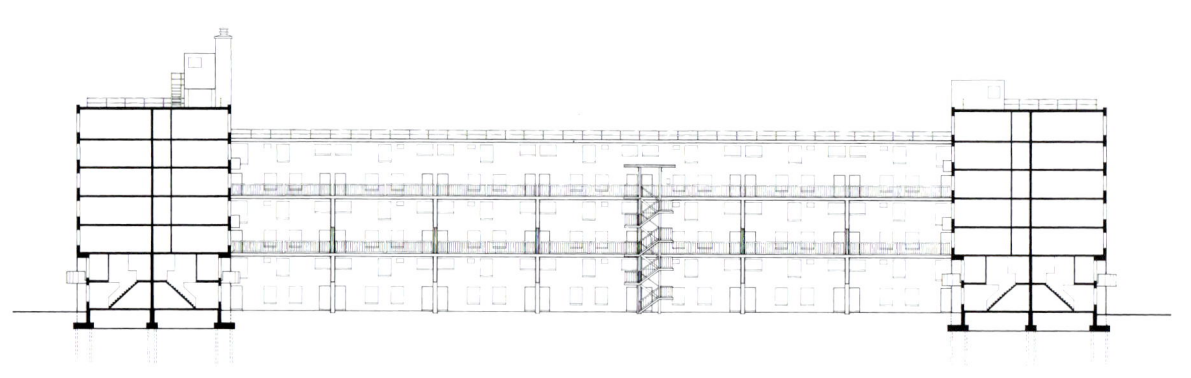

Above:
Although there are no fences, the building bars entrance to strangers.

Drawing:
Section

135

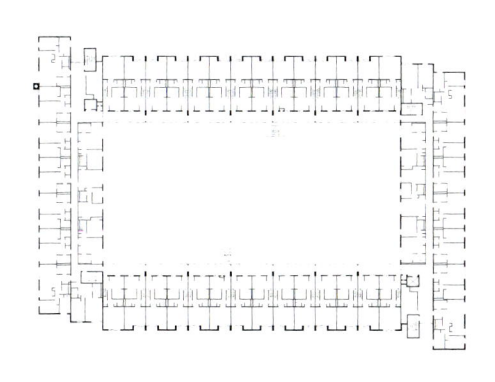

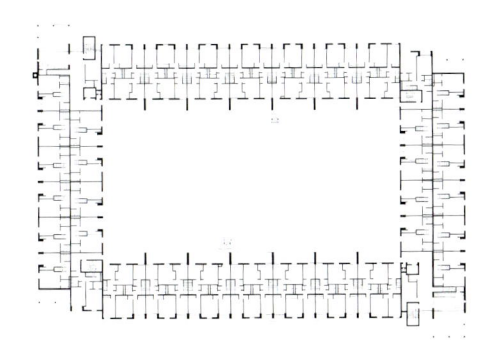

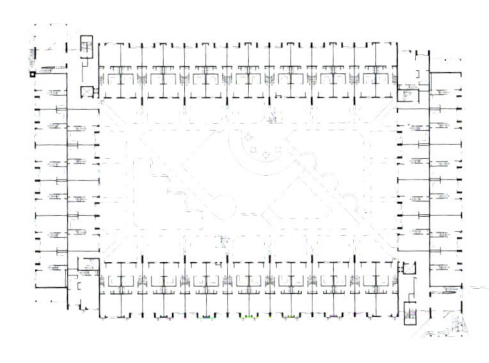

Drawings
bottom to top:
First, second, and
fifth floor plans

Above:
The courtyard is
visible from the
balconies.

136

Above:
Private exterior entrances of the first floor apartments establish visual continuity with the neighborhood.

Facing page:
Visitors are led into the building through a retracted corner.

137

Above left:
The balconies serve as entrances to the upper level duplexes.

Above right:
Three bedroom units have private gardens in the courtyard.

Facing page:
The courtyard provides a place where children can play in safety.

139

200 East 87th Street
New York, New York (1992)

200 East 87th Street is a triumph of physical structure dedicated to social function. Depending on who walks in, and through which doors, 200 East 87th Street is a collection of shops, a school, or home. Public retail spaces fill the first two floors; gymnasiums for the Dalton school, which act as semi-public spaces, reach from the third to the seventh floors; and private residential apartments occupy the eighth to the 22nd floors. John Ciardullo Associates tastefully met the primary design mandate: to secure the appropriate function, scale, and architectural demarcation for each section, and to do it within a reasonable budget.

The client, already holding a proposal from another firm, chose John Ciardullo Associates for John Ciardullo's experience and formal education in structural engineering as well as architecture. The competing firm's proposal, for a reinforced concrete structure, would have required huge, heavy transfer girders to allow for the large column-free spaces of the two stacked gymnasiums. Ciardullo reviewed these plans and redesigned the building using flat slab concrete construction on the retail floors and steel framing above. Analysis by The Steel Institute of New York vindicated Ciardullo's design. Ciardullo also indicated off-site fabrication of columns and beams known as "tree columns," which ensured higher quality welds, less down-time due to weather, and quicker erection than traditional column and beam construction. Ultimately, John Ciardullo Associates' redesign saved the client one million dollars in material and labor costs.

This building was one of the first steel and concrete plank residential buildings erected in New York City since the 1920s. Above the eighth floor, steel frames support pre-stressed concrete plates eight feet wide and eight inches thick. An unanticipated benefit of this reinstated method was that the client could now meet new zoning laws, requiring that high-rise buildings be stepped back from the setback line after reaching a height of 150 feet.

The redesign also made the building 30 percent lighter. The plate girders on the eighth floor that support the load of the residential floors are 70 feet long and 98 inches deep, with flanges only five by 33 inches. The substantial difference between these and the concrete girders of the original design, which would have been ten feet wide and nine feet long, saved on material and weight. Ciardullo also redesigned the wind frame, replacing the suggested concrete sheer walls with steel trusses. This is easier to manage with steel frame than with concrete frame construction.

200 East 87th Street challenged the architects in the complexity of the social functions it had to serve. Shoppers needed to feel free to enter and leave the public retail spaces on the lower floors, students using the gymnasiums had to see the site as part of their urban campus, and the residents of the upper floors needed to feel that this building was their home. The architects met the varying needs of each group by clearly indicating a position on the private-public continuum with brick detailing and window arrangements, as well as the stepped-back massing.

Residents and students enter the building on 87th Street, through the largest break in the brick cladding. The entrance opens onto a sumptuous lobby that repeats the identifying elements of the building's exterior: varied sizes of glass panels, a striking yet elegant color palette, terracing, and fine, solid materials, including black granite, terrazzo, and cherry. A lounge area on the fifth floor is considered a zoning ordinance incentive to the developer. This semi-private space is naturally illuminated by large façade windows and serves the entire residential community.

141

Above:
In accordance with zoning laws, the building is stepped back after 150 feet.

Those who call this building home do not feel as if they are holed up in a giant grid. The units vary in size from studio efficiencies to four-bedroom luxury units. Varied fenestration assigns the large corner windows to the public living spaces of the luxury apartments. Externally, horizontal lines of offset glazed brick accentuate the individuality and elegance of these corner units. Interrupting the horizontal detailing are vertical insets shooting up nine and 15 stories through both street-facing façades. This element visually defines the smaller central units without relegating them to anonymity within the large upper block. The stepped massing adds to the individual character of the residential floors, allowing more light to reach the street and rewarding tenants on every other floor with terraces at least seven feet wide.

The window proportions further counteract the visual effect of the building's true height, shrinking the scale of the experiences to those promised by the building's various functions. The public retail entrance is on 3rd Avenue, where it does not challenge the semi-public and private entrances. This space anchors the structure. Its two-story glass façades help counter the confusion inherent in a city street and invite shoppers to experience a controlled public space. These regular punctures in the brick are contrasted with the asymmetric windows demarcating the Dalton School space above. From within, the gymnasium windows admit light from a slice of glass near the ceiling, so as not to interfere with students' vision during sports. The floors between the public retail spaces and the private residential spaces are of a semi-public nature, justifying the playful distribution of windows on the façade. This sprinkling of distinct shapes invites those heading toward the building to identify the various interior spaces even from some distance down the street.

In 200 East 87th Street, John Ciardullo Associates successfully designed three separate spaces with separate functions for separate populations. By visualizing the problem from the social perspective and then choosing the appropriate materials and technologies, the firm produced a strong architectural manifestation of those functions and populations.

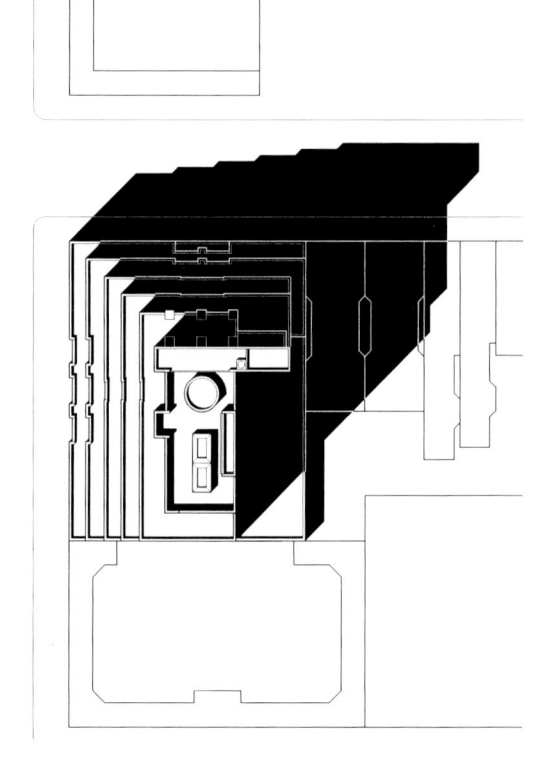

Drawing:
Site plan

Above left: Horizontal lines of offset brick accent corner units.

Above right: Vertical insets, shooting up nine and 15 stories, interrupt the horizontal detailing.

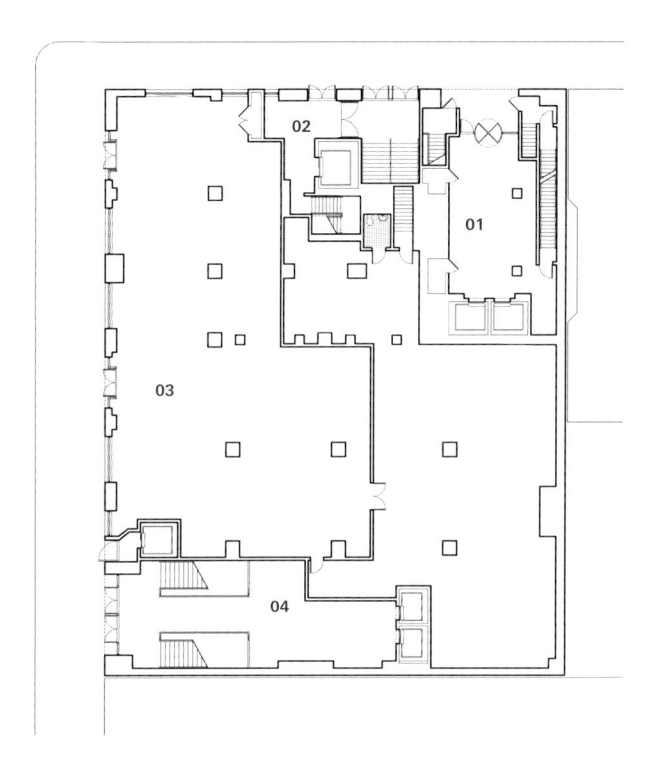

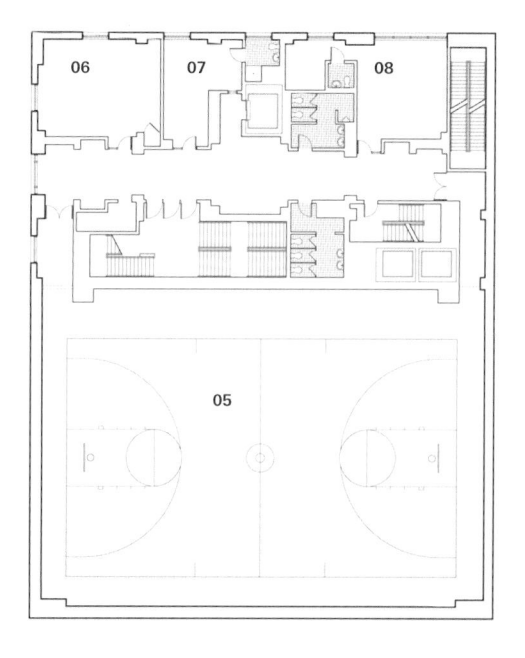

144

01.	02.	03.	04.	05.	06.	07.	08.
Entrance to the residential building	**Entrance to the school gymnasium**	**Ground floor retail**	**Entrance to second and basement floor retail**	**Gymnasium**	**Wrestling room**	**Office**	**Entrance**

**Above left to right:
First and second
floor plans**

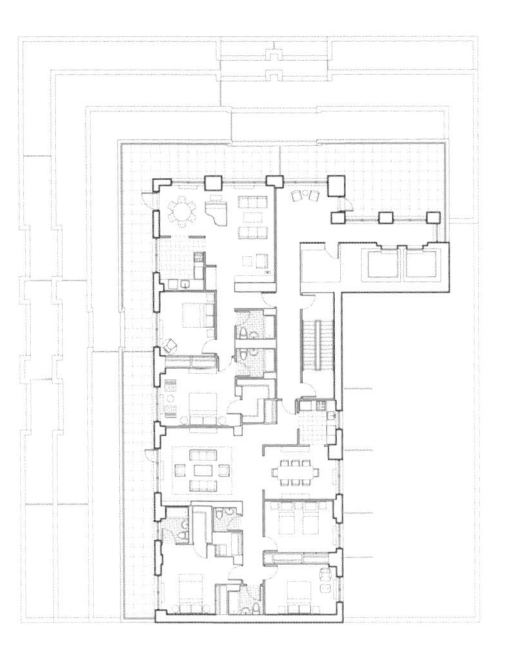

Above left:
Typical residential
floors eighth -
17th plan.

Above right:
Penthouse level
plan

146

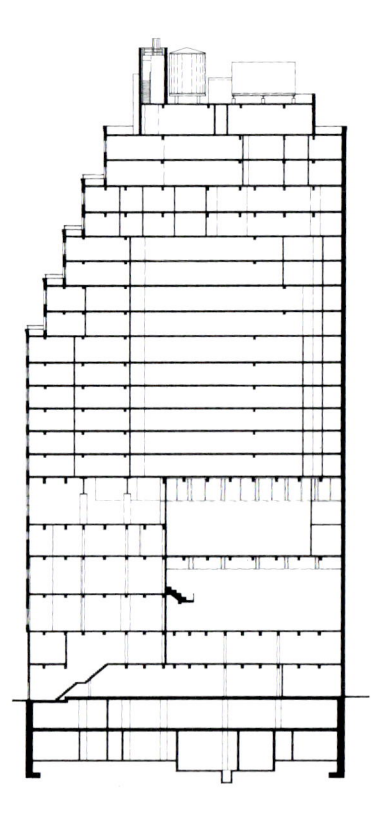

Drawing:
Section

Above:
The varied fenestration demarcates the building's various functions.

All above:
The residential lobby, school gymnasium, and residential community room are all semi-private spaces for the building's inhabitants.

147

148 Planned Communities

"The residents of planned communities choose to live in this social grouping, and in a safer, more private community. They experience life in a community where there is a commonality of materials, aesthetics, and circulation. The requirement of a public access way indicates an area where they may meet exterior neighbors. However, you, the architect, are always controlling where they can interact."

John Ciardullo

Port Regalle
Staten Island, New York (1988)

In planned communities, the site—a specific, existing neighborhood with its own social setting and demography—is the public parameter. The architect must define private space and individuality within that. The community he or she designs must encompass this individuality, link the residences to one another, and link the new community to the existing neighborhood. On the shores of Staten Island, the Port Regalle waterfront community stands in a diverse residential and commercial neighborhood. It satisfies its residents' dual desires for the privacy of single-family dwellings and the luxurious experience of the vast Atlantic environment. The complex includes an exclusive 300-slip marina in the protected cove of Great Kills Harbor, with some of the finest fishing waters in the Northeast.

In Port Regalle, John Ciardullo Associates aimed for and achieved the ideal balance between privacy and expanse for each resident, whether he or she chooses a one-bedroom unit with a sleeping loft or a three-bedroom unit with a tower reached by a spiral staircase. Each of the 340 units on the 38-acre site has the amenities of both resorts and private homes: a separate entrance, a private garden, and its own garage. The density, 17 units per acre, is relatively high for the area, but the effect of the unique interlocking units and rambling, climbing architecture gives a sense of community that is far from stifling. The varying levels, soaring towers, and stepping terraces give the community the appearance of a Mediterranean hillside village that evolved across the land over time.

In keeping with this image, the architects visually unified the exterior by using tile roofs of Mediterranean red and salmon-colored stucco finish. They determined circulation and interior design using social, not formal, criteria. The layout of the site provides the comfort of the controlled social experience that residents seek in a planned community. Opposing entrances mean that residents enter their private dwellings without a sense of living above or below anyone else. All of the units offer open living spaces designed to take advantage of the view of the open sky and sea. To accentuate the privacy of each unit, the architects created private gardens. From these, residents can access the semi-public communal gardens and seating areas, the marina walkway, and the public promenade.

To enforce privacy for the entire community, the architects limited vehicle access to roads ending in cul-de-sacs that serve the units' garages and entrances. The ocean-side entrance to the complex is complemented by three controlled entries, and the buildings themselves physically shield the community's sedate gardens and walkways from the busy parking areas. In the fens, or common space leading to the water, residents can stroll without ever seeing an automobile. The boardwalk, following the shoreline, allows access to the precious water environment and reconnects the Port Regalle community with its surroundings.

Port Regalle offers an unparalleled opportunity for New York City residents to enjoy the privacy of a single family home while reveling in a unique connection to their ocean-side community and environment.

Facing page:
The complex includes an exclusive 300-slip marina.

151

152

Left:
Along the public path to the water, residents can stroll without ever seeing a car.

Middle:
Vehicle access is limited to roads leading to cul-de-sacs.

Right:
The boardwalk allows access to Great Kills Cove.

153

154

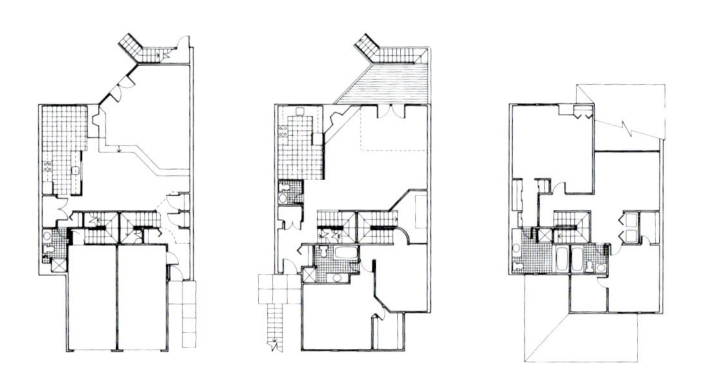

**Drawings
botton to top:
Unit A, B, and C plans**

All above:
The open living spaces take advantage of the sky and sea.

156

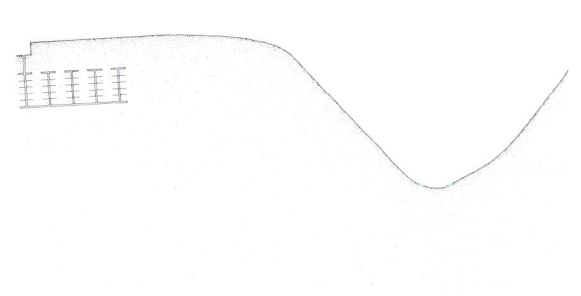

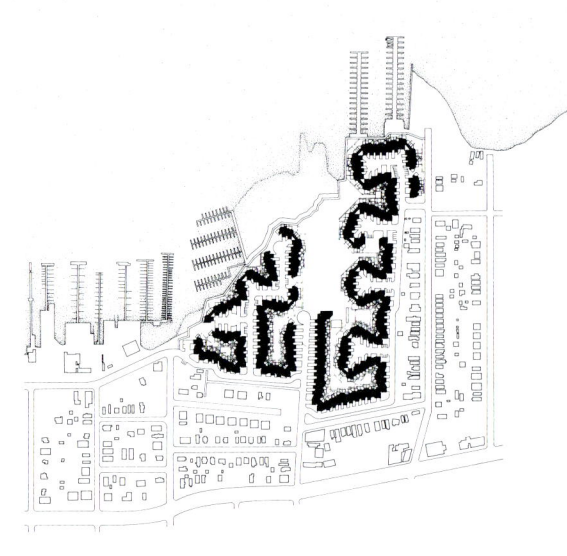

Above:
Private gardens separate units from the walkways along the cove.

Drawing:
Site plan

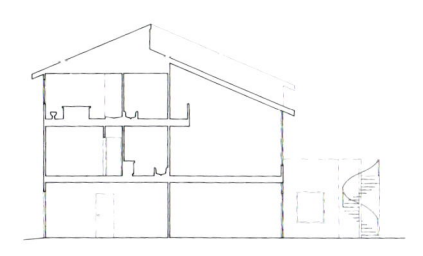

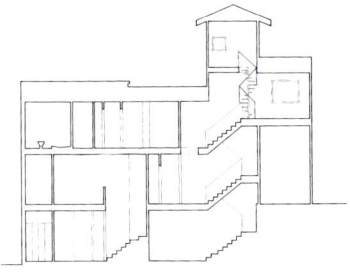

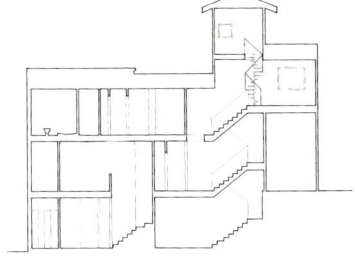

Drawings bottom to top: Unit B, C, and A sections

Above: Mediterranean red tile roofs and salmon stucco finish unify the exterior.

157

Rock Shelter Road
Waccabuc, New York (1998)

Rock Shelter Road is a 102-acre site in the hamlet of Waccabuc in New York's northeastern Westchester County. It is John Ciardullo's answer to the needs of a particular set of clients at the turn of the 21st century. These clients, many of whom moved to Waccabuc from urban centers, need privacy but also the security of a community for their families. There are 21 four-acre sites on Rock Shelter Road, for which John Ciardullo Associates designs, engineers, develops, and builds traditionally styled custom homes. Although the price point for this community is higher than that of John Ciardullo Associates' other planned communities and multi-family housing, the overriding concern remains that the new properties and community be socially and architecturally integrated with an existing social and physical neighborhood.

The firm's concern with the financial bottom line is evident even here. John Ciardullo Associates' unique design/build approach eliminates the pitfalls of conventional owner-coordinated custom-home projects, in which the owner buys land and then hires architects and contractors separately, and fixtures and finishes are considered price-boosting upgrades. In Rock Shelter Road, refined hand finishing of carpentry and ceramics, and superior interior amenities are included in the price of a home. The firm maintains a no-changes policy, unless the client specifically requests upgrades. The common material palette of Rock Shelter homes—stone bases, cedar roofs, exposed fireplaces of indigenous stone, and wood trim—affiliates all the residents, who share not only space, but social aspirations.

Developing Rock Shelter Road tested the tenacity of John Ciardullo Associates. One of six major lake communities in Lewisboro, Waccabuc was settled more than 200 years ago and boasts a population that actively preserves the community. The landowners' association maintains the local post office and holds various community events. For 12 years, Ciardullo discussed his plan with the town board for integrating custom-built, traditionally styled homes into the community, which would preclude architectural discrepancy. In developing this new community, the architects overlooked no opportunity to add to the area's distinctive pastoral charm. Every architectural and landscaping move was a considered mechanism to integrate Rock Shelter Road into the greater community.

Before beginning development, John Ciardullo Associates conducted archeological research, which revealed an ancient rock shelter. This now marks the entrance to Rock Shelter Road—the first and most symbolic physical manifestation of the environmentally aware social community that Ciardullo has added to Waccabuc. The architects insisted that the road, while new, remain unpaved, narrow (20 feet, rather than the standard 24), uncurbed, and lined with fieldstone walls, thus maintaining the whole area as an intrinsically rural environment while connecting the new community to Waccabuc. To site the homes and install septic systems, the architects felled as few trees as possible, and have discouraged residents from fencing their properties. Much of the community land abuts horse trails and other public land, such as the Long Pond Reserve, formed in 1970 and owned by the Nature Conservancy, to which Ciardullo donated eight acres.

Above:
An ancient rock shelter, the development's namesake, sits nearby the entry from Chapel Road.

Drawing:
Site plan

159

160

161

Facing and all above:
John Ciardullo Associates
designs, engineers,
develops, and builds
traditionally styled
custom homes for the
development.

Private Homes

"Essentially, private homes are an enclave for the family; interaction beyond the family is only encouraged through the streets. On extra-urban sites like these, the exterior social context is less in evidence than in urban areas or planned communities. And the rural setting makes the treatment of the natural context much more important. When you design a house in rough terrain, you don't want to decimate the land for the house. You want to reach a symbiotic balance so that house and land uniquely fit together as if the house not only belongs there but has been there forever."

John Ciardullo

Ciardullo House
Pleasantville, New York (1971)

John Ciardullo completed this private home in Pleasantville, New York in 1971, a year after founding John Ciardullo Associates at the age of 30. The 90-foot trees that fill the site indicate the age of the area, an area that called to Ciardullo as the site of Frank Lloyd Wright's Usonian Development homes, just outside the village of Pleasantville. But it was the "walking village" aspect of the town that offered Ciardullo his dream: a community.

John Ciardullo grew up in a family of four, in a one-bedroom apartment in the Bronx. His apartment building was opposite and flanked by properties owned by his grandfather and occupied by relatives. He was always impressed with the concept of privacy and the comfort of a family in its community. Having never lived in a house (as a child he slept in the living room of his family's urban apartment building), Ciardullo strove to live not simply on the land, but in constant appreciation of its breadth, and of the ordered participation of humanity in a village. The Ciardullo house describes John Ciardullo's unique relationship to his surroundings, both natural and manmade.

The site presented two overriding challenges: the steeply sloping hillside demanded a potent relationship to the land, and its position behind two already built parcels immediately raised the question of the new home's relationship to neighboring properties, as well as the new relationship among the families living there. Ciardullo liberated the site with a thoughtful design that delicately balances a contemporary three-story structure along the hillside, and presents a generous countenance to the neighborhood.

The two-story façade of the entrance approach is clad in vertical cedar siding, relating to the heavily wooded, 3/4-acre site. This façade is broken by a breezeway connecting the front entrance with the garage. This void in an otherwise solid façade provides a dramatic view of the crest of the hill, emphasizing the tenuous balance of the house on the hill. The materials palette of white painted brick, cedar siding, and glass relates to the natural terrain, vertical growth, and open sky. The site is finally connected to the public street by a strip of land 15 feet wide.

The L-shaped house flows seamlessly down the hill. Extending terraces, floating balconies, and stepping forms connect the complex interior spaces with the densely wooded site. The volumetric relationship of solid forms and open voids creates a lively interplay that dissolves the boundaries between inside and outside spaces.

Expansive windows indicate the public space within the house, an open living/dining room that projects out over the hill. The kitchen, grounding the entry level, both draws the eye to the outside vista through a private terrace and offers a retreat to the lower level via a spiral staircase. In contrast to the straight lines of the surrounding trees, the circular element is comforting. It echoes the tree trunks and is repeated in the semi-circular vertical stair tower connecting the family area on the lower level and the living/dining rooms on the upper level. The same curve is repeated on the extremity of the deck reaching out from the dining room.

Achieving the perfect balance between private and public space, the bedrooms, semi-private spaces on the upper floor, face south and feature unobstructed views of the hillside. The master bedroom most effectively stretches the limits of both kinds of space with a 15-foot-wide sliding glass door that opens onto an east-facing terrace.

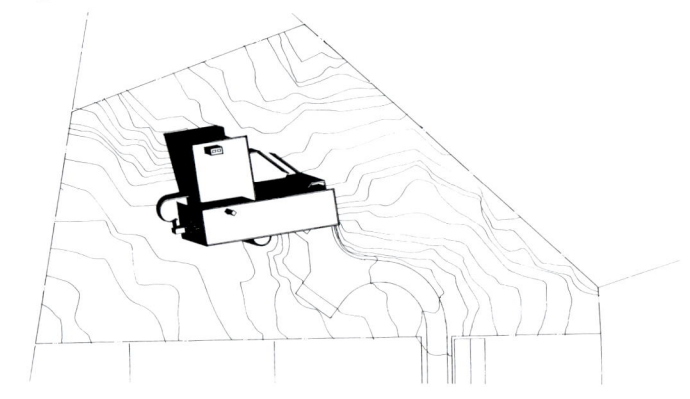

Facing page:
The façade is broken by a breezeway connecting the front entrance with the garage.

Drawing:
Site plan

165

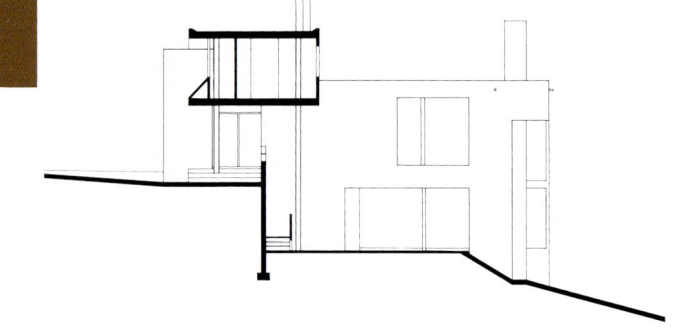

Above left:
The main entrance in the breezeway is protected from the elements.

Drawing:
Section

Above right:
The volumetric relationship of solid forms and open voids creates a lively interplay.

Facing page:
The cedar siding and glass relate to the natural environment.

167

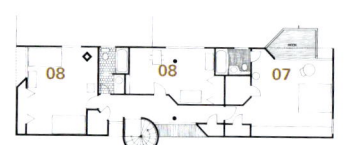

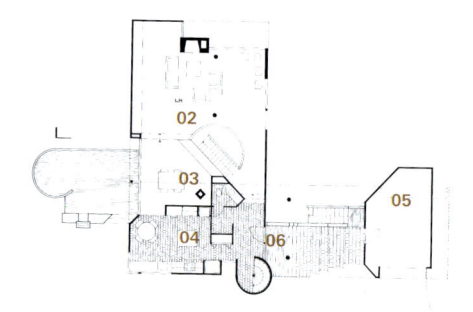

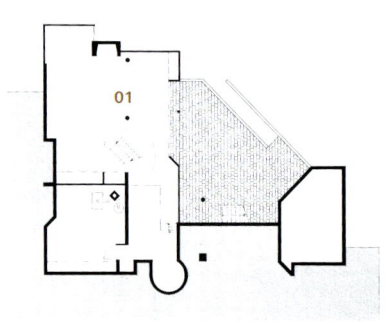

01.
Family room

02.
Living room

03.
Dining room

04.
Kitchen

05.
Garage

06.
Foyer

07.
Master bedroom

08.
Bedrooms

Above:
An outdoor terrace extends off the kitchen and dining room.

Drawings bottom to top: lower, entry, and upper level plans

Facing page:
The circular stair tower relates to the surrounding tree trunks.

169

170

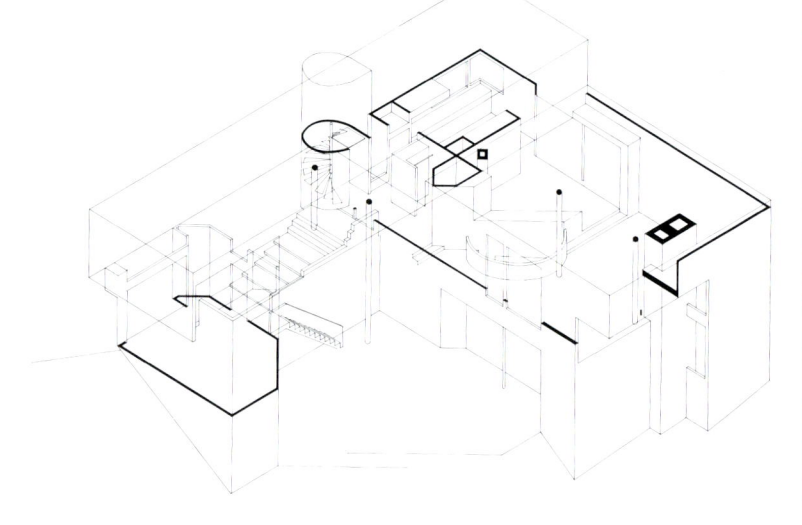

Drawing:
Isometric

Above:
Living and family room windows face south, allowing for passive solar heating.

Above:
From the living room a view leads through the breezeway to the front yard.

172

173

Facing page:
Living, dining, and kitchen areas flow into one another.

Above left:
A circular opening links the entry level with the lower level.

Above right:
A living/family room is provided on the lower level.

Perless House
Greenwich, Connecticut (1982)

Contrast is the theme of the Perless residence. John Ciardullo Associates was commissioned to design a studio and residence/gallery for the modernist metal sculptor Robert Perless on a rugged six-acre site in Greenwich, Connecticut. The geometric volumes, materials, and colors of the all-synthetic house declare the industrial, functional, and modernist aspects of the artist's preferences and sculptural work. The landscape replies with the irregularities of nature. The powerful presence and refined finish of the semi-public living area and gallery are thrown into relief by the contrasting eroded volume at the corner, which leaves a single, slender column to support the overhanging roof. Inside, one moves through the house, downward with the slope of the ravine, while the glass walls, 30 feet wide and 26 feet high, direct attention upward to branches and the open sky.

Because the 6,500-square-foot building had to act as a gallery for metal sculptures and mobiles as well as a manufacturing facility and living space, Ciardullo defined the private aspect of the house on the exterior with a singular curved shell surrounding the second-floor master bedroom. The open, geometric, glassed, and predominantly anodized aluminum public aspect of the structure is opposed by the strictly private space, the master bedroom suite. This suite, cantilevered over the living room, remains hidden from interior views. It is connected by both stair and bridge to the first floor, and faces outward to the 50-foot ravine, pond, and stand of oaks below. The living area is dominated by the sculptor's kinetic "Hanging White Mobile," and features all built-in furniture, except for the Breuer chairs. In contrast to this static setting, Perless' sculpture is set in rotating motion by air currents moving though the house.

The table and hearth, custom-designed and finished with the same abrasion-resistant paint as is used on aircraft and on the artist's sculptures, evoke the public atmosphere of a gallery or museum, as does the color palette, limited to metallic, gray, white, and black. Ciardullo accomplished the vast expanse necessary to fully enjoy Perless' work by using materials from the artist's world. Echoing the stark dynamic forms of the exterior, the living room attains a clear span of 25 feet and a height of 26 feet by means of steel columns, metal joists, and steel studs. The adjoining studio, with 20-foot ceilings, has a clear span totaling 40 feet. These uninterrupted and austere interior spaces flow through the glass panels to establish visual and volumetric links to the outdoors.

In the Perless residence, the artist's familiarity with materials and involvement in the process clarified construction and complemented Ciardullo's design. Interior materials are manmade: gray acrylic carpet, stainless steel kitchen countertops, black synthetic rubber flooring, aluminum railings and cabinet doors, and a steel mantelpiece. The exterior is coated with panels of Alucobond, a core of polyethylene secured between sheets of anodized aluminum, each hand cut by Perless himself, insuring the precision evident in the sculptural work displayed inside. Perless also built the custom aluminum panels that wrap the house.

The union of art and architecture and the demarcation of private and public spaces are powerfully stated in the Perless residence. The presence of this refined object in the landscape clearly defines the separation between the natural and the man-made, calling attention to both and their relationship in proximity.

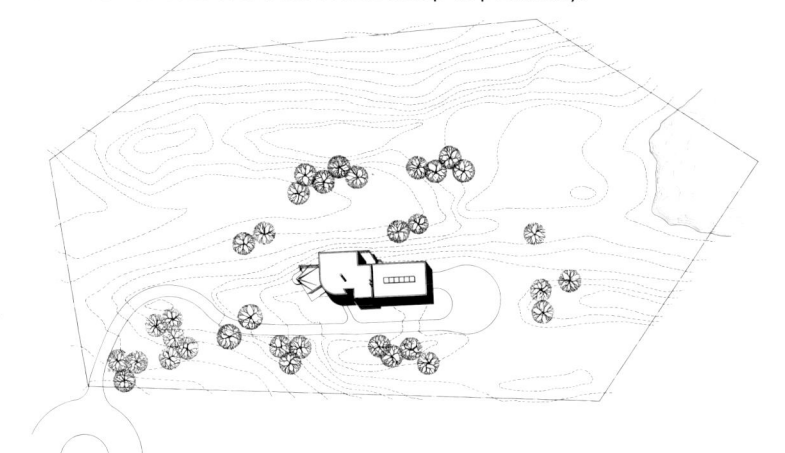

Facing page:
The living space opens to the landscape through a two-story glass curtainwall.

Drawings:
Site plan

175

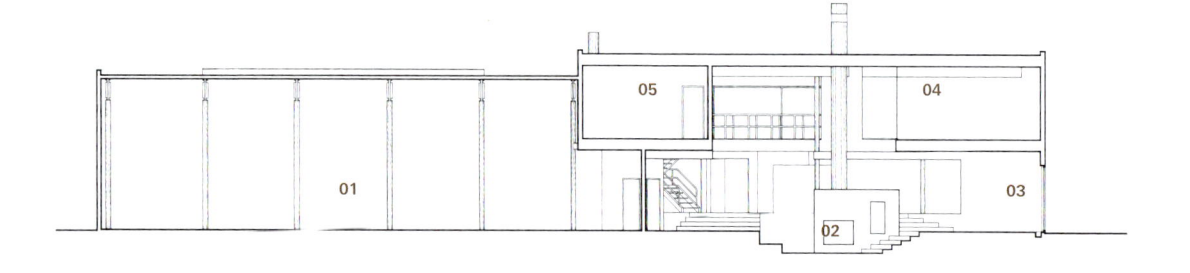

01.	02.	03.	04.	05.
Studio	Living room	Dining room	Master bedroom	Bedroom

Left:
The hard lines of the architecture contrast with the irregularities of the landscape.

Middle:
One of Perless' sculptures greets visitors coming up the driveway

Drawing:
Section

Right:
The house cantilevers over a ravine.

177

Above left:
A singular curved shell covers the second floor master bedroom.

Above right:
Views from the entrance stair lead directly to the living room.

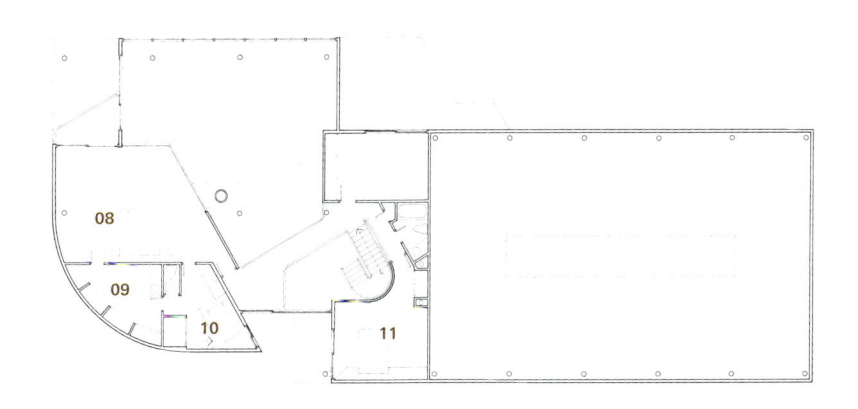

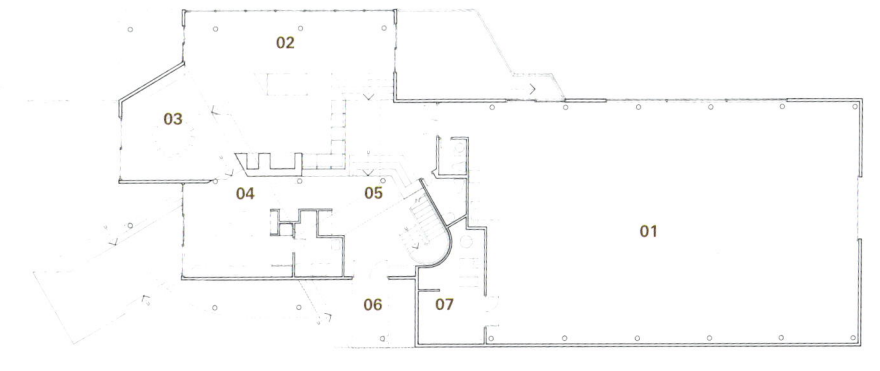

01. Studio	02. Living room	03. Dining room	04. Kitchen	05. Foyer	06. Entrance	07. Storage and mechanical room	08. Master bedroom
09. Closet	10. Master bathroom	11. Bedroom	Drawings bottom to top: First and second floor plans				

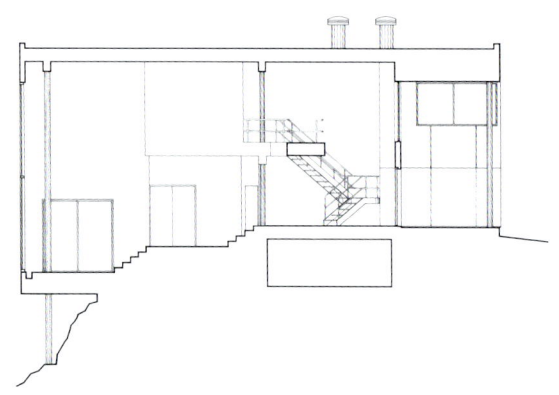

Above left:
The table and hearth are finished with the same abrasion-resistant paint used on aircraft.

Drawing:
Section

Above right:
Air currents moving through the house set the Perless mobile in circular motion.

Facing page:
The master bedroom suite cantilevers over the living room.

181

Browne House
Waccabuc, New York (1990)

The Browne House is as a weekend home for a lawyer and his wife, who had lived in an apartment in the Central Park West section of New York City for many years. They wanted to expand their experience of nature, to feel a part of the forest on their six-acre plot in Westchester County. The site slopes steeply in two directions, and is punctuated by a number of large rock outcroppings.

Using this gradation as an indication of the most appropriate way to order the spaces on the private-public continuum, John Ciardullo Architects nested a clapboard enclosure into the hill, with the entry, kitchen, and dining area on the first level and bedrooms and baths on the second. The result is a warm and comforting space for the family. The bedrooms and baths on the second level are tucked over the kitchen, but are expanded by a demi-study cantilevered ten feet into the living room. The bedrooms open onto outdoor terraces at the top of the hill, which are sheltered by partial stone walls. On the opposing, lower side of the site, the experience is practically ethereal; the family room is a grand glass pavilion thrusting 25 feet up into the sky.

Rising from a high, sturdy base of stone quarried from the site, the house appears to have emerged from its natural surroundings. The kitchen and breakfast area, nestled firmly into the hill, are opposed slightly by a semi-public dining area, bounded by a passageway carved out below by a curving stone wall, and above by a waving flag of the traditional shelter material of clapboard. Between these is an undulating ribbon of glass wall. The curving colonnade allows for two possible nooks where the family can sit together. And so, figuratively as well as literally, through this corridor illuminated by the sun, the family passes from its private to public spaces.

In this 5,100-square-foot home, John Ciardullo Associates followed the contingencies of the site to create a comfortable harmony of unique spaces that allow a family to enjoy every level of privacy and unity, and to commune with the magnitude of nature.

Facing page:
Rising from a sturdy base of local stone, the house appears to have emerged from the natural surroundings.

Drawing:
Site plan

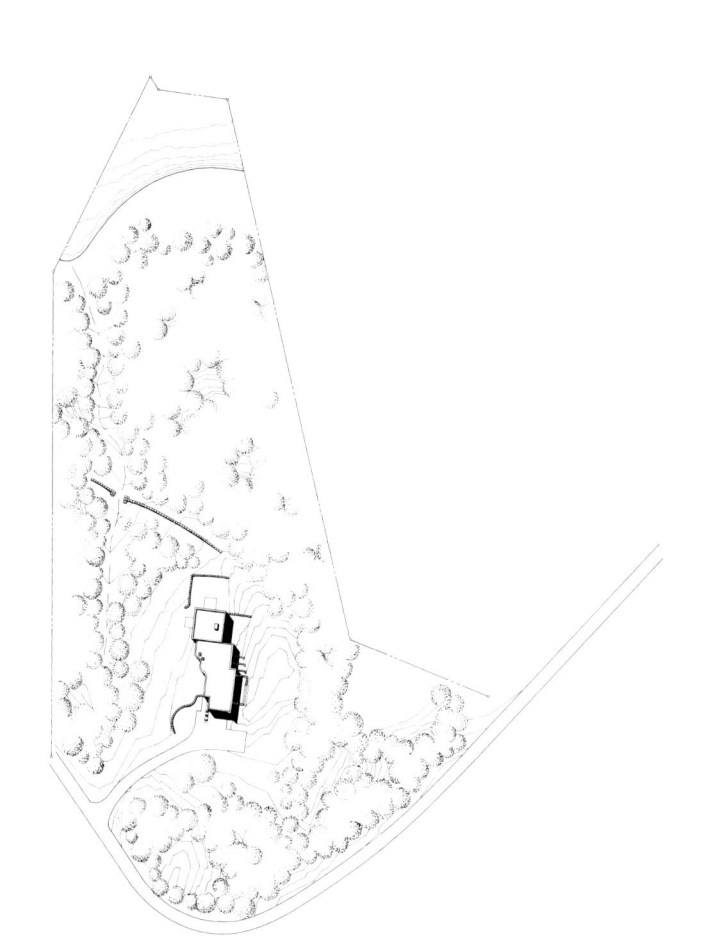

183

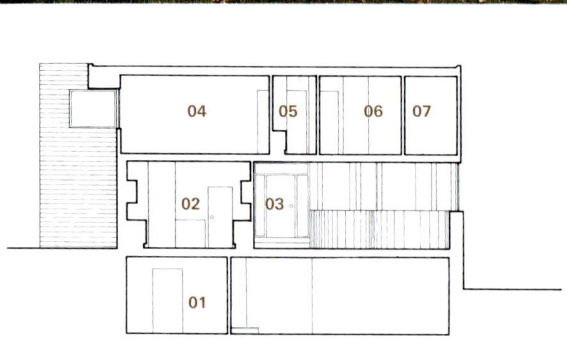

01.	02.	03.	04.	05.	06.	07.
Storage	Kitchen	Dining room	Master bedroom	Dressing room	Master bathroom	Hall

Above Left:
The undulating wall of stone, glass, and clapboard provides nooks where the family can sit.

Drawing:
Section

Middle:
The garage creates a formal boundary between private and public space.

Right:
From the entry the view looks directly through dining and living rooms.

Above:
A terrace expands
from the living room
and kitchen.

187

01. Family room
02. Living room
03. Master bedroom
04. Entrance foyer
05. Dining room
06. Balcony

Drawing: Section

Above left: A 25-foot glass pavilion encloses the living room.

Above right: The kitchen is nestled into the hill.

01.	02.	03.	04.	05.	06.	07.	08.
Family room	Guest room	Mechanical room	Living room	Dining area	Kitchen	Foyer	Garage

Drawings left to right: Lower and entry level plans.

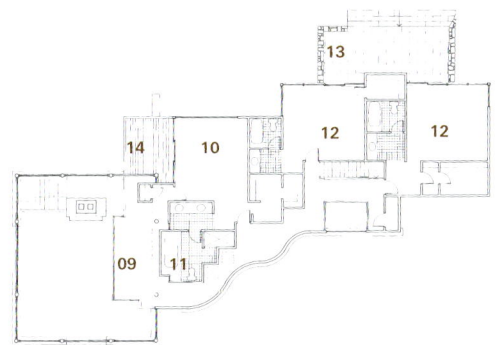

09.
Balcony

10.
Master bedroom

11.
Master bath

12.
Bedrooms

13.
Terrace

14.
Master bedroom balcony

Drawing:
Upper level plan

Facing page left:
The house rises out of the sloping site.

Facing page right:
The family room is on a lower level.

All above:
The living room is a soaring, light-filled space.

Torres House
Waccabuc, New York (1993)

The Torres house was created as a speculative home on a two-and-a-half-acre wooded site next to the entrance of John Ciardullo's as-yet-unbuilt Rock Shelter Road development. Answering only to the parameters of the natural surroundings and the imagination, Ciardullo created a home that is both sculptural and natural, both private and inviting. The program required that the house be sheltered from further residential development, and that it accommodate four-bedrooms as well as an au pair suite that would appeal to many potential buyers. Ciardullo designed the garage at a right angle to the road, and faced it with stone, making it compatible with the stone walls common to the area and formally sympathetic to the dramatic rock outcroppings on the site. A soaring two-story archway between the garage and the house marks the entrance and acts as a portal from the public entry side and the private landscaped patio beyond. A semi-circular stair tower is the organic axis that anchors the geometric forms. The main house is sided in a grey-white vertical cedar, which both imitates the surrounding trees and clarifies this beautiful modern form that backs the woods.

Inside, the first-floor public spaces contract in size, from the two-story glassed living room, to the more intimate dining room. Sweeping bluestone patios and manicured lawns echo the open atmosphere of the living areas, and a rugged two-story stone fireplace in the living room replies to the more finished stone of the landscaping. The large family room and au pair suite on the lower level, which is carved into the side of the hill, open out onto a separate bluestone patio.

The upper level is demarcated as a private space and holds all the bedrooms, with the master bedroom suite overlooking the living room. The master bedroom has access to a private terrace with unique views of the wooded forest, further blurring the boundaries between interior and exterior, while maintaining the division of public and private experiences. The lower level contains a family room with direct access to grade by the natural sloping site.

Facing page: The circular balconies anchor the house's geometric forms.

Drawing:
Site plan

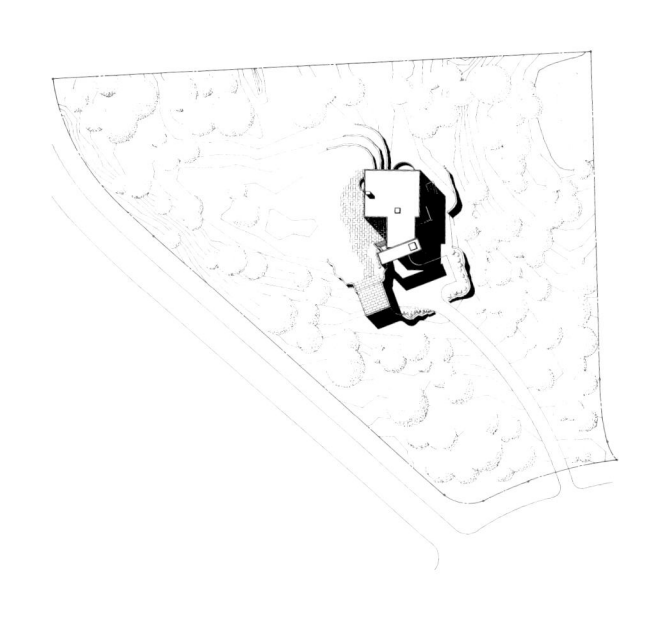

191

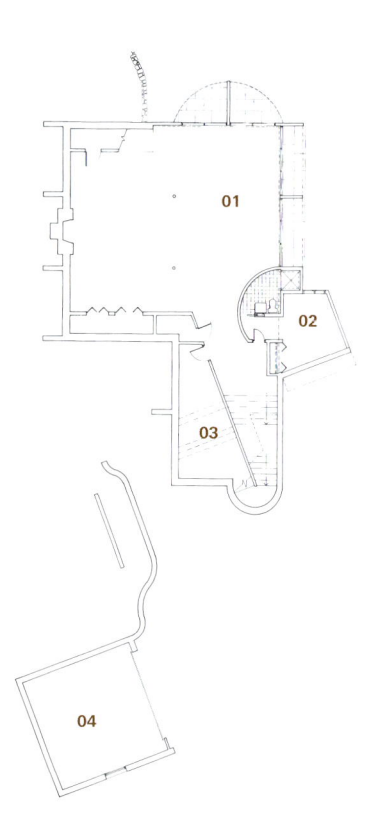

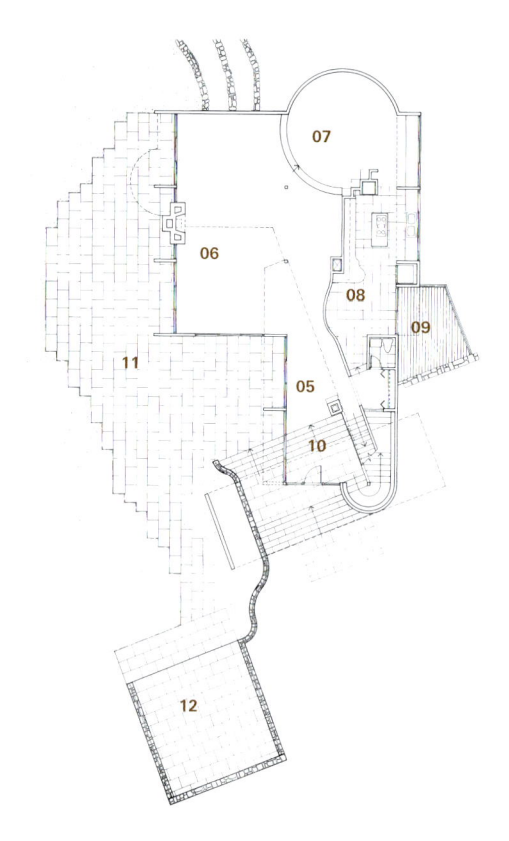

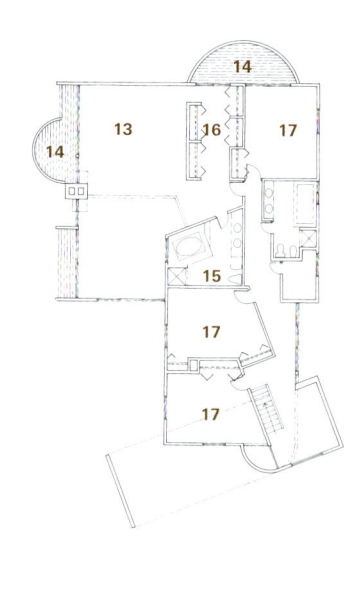

01. Family room	02. Guest bedroom	03. Mechanical room	04. Garage	05. Foyer	06. Living room	07. Dining room	08. Kitchen
09. Kitchen balcony	10. Entrance	11. Patio	12. Terrace over garage	13. Master bedroom	14. Master balconies	15. Master bath	16. Closet
17. Bedrooms							

Drawings
left to right:
lower, entry, and
upper levels

All above:
A two-story archway between the garage and house marks the entry.

193

Above left:
A sweeping bluestone terrace reaches out from the living areas.

Below left:
The master bedroom is outfitted with a private balcony.

Middle:
A terrace above the garage is level with the house.

Right:
The garage is faced with stone common to the area.

Samberg House
Chappaqua, New York (2001)

Here, as in many of his private homes, Ciardullo explored the boundaries between private space, where the members of a family retreat to be alone; semi-private space, where a family gathers together; semi-public space, where a family accepts others into its environment; and public space, represented by the landscape outside the home. Even when it was first built in the 1920s, the Samberg house was meant for entertaining, and thus was designed to be more public than private. The client purchased the property for the rambling space and for the magnificent view it already offered of the New York City skyline. John Ciardullo Associates was commissioned to expand and alter the structure and grounds to accommodate more guests, allow for more outdoor activities, and enhance the experience of living atop one of the highest points in Westchester County.

The original home, a private, cozy structure of stone and wood, was entered through a covered stone patio at the basement level. To solve the problem of reaching the first floor, the architects created a raised entry in a campanile between the original home and the addition, accessed by a gently climbing terraced staircase. This tower focuses and resolves the entrance, clearly delineating the new portion from the original. The original dining room was re-appointed as a living room, and the original kitchen as a foyer. The campanile serves as an entry foyer.

The client's lifestyle and hobbies anticipated a ten-car garage, extensive exercise room, private rear-projection screening room, private guest suite, and deluxe master changing rooms and baths, all of which are expansive spaces. The client, however, also wanted the space to function as a typical house, with a very informal living room, kitchen, and breakfast room. Once the architects had replaced the original dining room with a living room, the formal dining room had to be relocated. They designed a transitional gallery off of the campanile that would draw guests into a formal dining room as well as satisfy the client's need for space to display a growing collection of art and sculpture.

In a house designed for entertaining and long-term visits from friends, independence is as important as camaraderie. Although both guests and family members sleep on the second floor, family members climb the stairs in the original home, while guests use the stairs in the addition. A two-story living room separates the guest suite from the family area on the second floor.

In the addition, the architects used traditional and modern materials to harmonize and balance the two sections. In the new, more public side, the warmth of the original structure is echoed by Jerusalem stone in the drive and on the living room floor, French roof stone in the guest suite, and wood flooring throughout. In contrast, on the first floor the architects created a state-of-the-art exercise room with white steel beams and chrome track lighting that extend through a curtainwall looking out on the New York City skyline. The balcony railing is clean white steel tubing.

Situated on the slope behind the house is a pool high enough to give bathers a view of the city skyline, unobstructed by the roofline of the house. In a minor alteration of the pool and its patio, the latter of which is slated as an outdoor sculpture garden, the architects repeated the curve of charming stone arches that extend from either side of the campanile.

The architects contrived site-work and landscaping to create dual water elements above (the pool) and below (a Jacuzzi on an outdoor patio). The material palette of the house is echoed by brick used in a changing room and mechanical room that were originally finished in stucco. These stand between the pool and the site of the new tennis courts, above the pool. In deference to the Italian architect who designed the original house and to his own ethnic heritage, Ciardullo reconstructed the original eight-pool waterfall flowing down to the pool and flanked it with an Italian staircase terminating in an ideal vantage point from which to survey the property.

**Facing page:
The original house, built in the 20s, was a cozy stone, brick, and wood structure.**

197

Left:
The curve of the charming stone arches is repeated in the pool.

Middle:
The pool is raised up high enough to afford a view of the Hudson River and New York City.

Right:
The entry tower links the existing structure with the new.

199

200

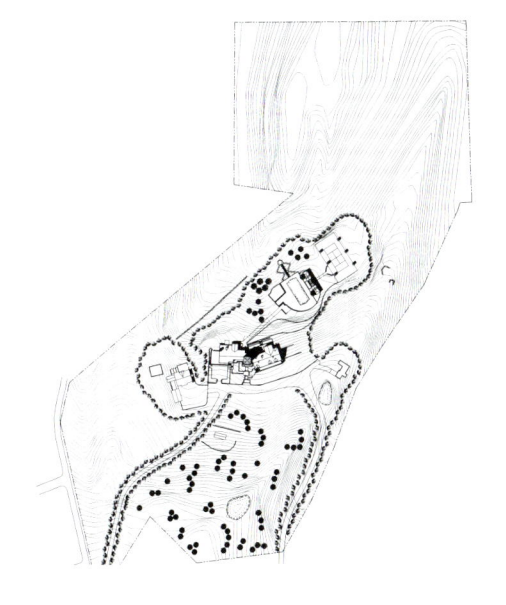

Facing page:
The new entry was raised to the first floor.

All above:
Both modern and traditional materials were used to harmonize the two sections.

Drawing:
Site plan

Above left:
The Hudson River Valley is visible from the breakfast room.

Above right:
The foyer is located in the old kitchen.

Facing page:
The recreation room is meant for entertaining.

Drawings bottom to top: lower, entry, and upper level plans

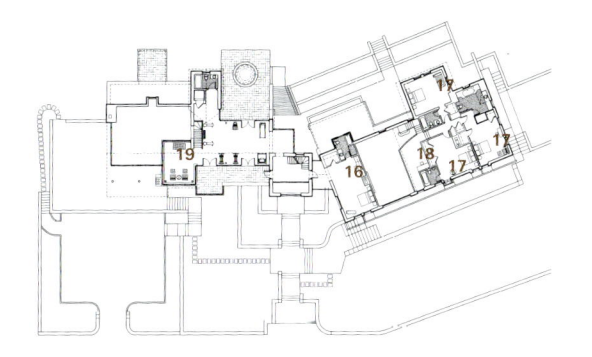

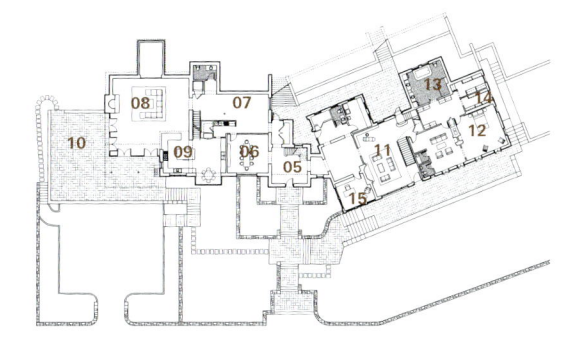

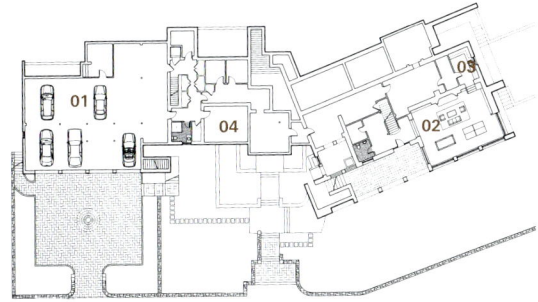

01. Garage	02. Recreation room	03. Recreation kitchen	04. Wine cellar	05. Foyer	06. Dining room	07. Gallery	08. Family room
09. Kitchen, breakfast room, and terrace	10. Terrace over garage	11. Living room	12. Master bedroom suite	13. Master bath	14. Master closet and dressing room	15. Office	16. Guest bedroom
			17. Bedrooms	18. Balcony over living room	19. Exercise room and office		

Corporate Interiors

"When you're designing a corporate space you have to understand not only the company, but the people. A successful corporate space is not just an office with people stuffed in desks, but a community...where they can talk about issues, about the work. Somebody has an idea on one thing, and somebody else adds his opinion...that kind of brings people together. The individual has his private space, his office. This is his domain. It can be sealed acoustically by shutting the door, and opened visually by using windows. The private-public continuum is expressed in a corporate interior within the parameters of the corporate culture. This particular client wants each employee to have a sense of the whole, and the freedom to interact with other employees in both labor and leisure pursuits."

John Ciardullo

Dawson Giammalva Capital Management, Inc.
Southport, Connecticut (1997)

In a corporate space, which is more public than any housing, but more private than any space with civic functions, the population is fixed. Fundamentally, employees are connected merely by similar occupations and a shared employer. How close-knit the group becomes depends on what kind of social environment the physical environment can support.

This money management firm began its business in a 150-year-old wood-framed mill house and complex in Southport, Connecticut. Its work demands that employees maintain open communication channels, whether in the semi-public environment of a trading room or the relative privacy of an office. The site was initially 2,500 square feet. Over several years the company expanded to the point that it required a strongly cohesive office covering three floors and 22,000 square feet.

Ultimately John Ciardullo Associates tied three stories together by creating an expansive environment using conspicuous open circulation, a unified materials palette, and light colors. Traditionally styled, wooden floored stairways with curving wooden banisters connect the various levels of the office. New partitions have wood stud walls. The elements of the original structure that imparted an informal atmosphere were also maintained: original wood trusses, natural maple floors, exposed brick walls, and exposed heating and sprinkler pipes.

With interaction as the theme and purpose of the architecture, John Ciardullo Associates established an airy interior conference room midway between the second and third floors of an adjacent structure with a clear span of 1,600 square feet. Talking together in this room, which is illuminated by natural light that pours through a domed skylight, employees connect in the comfort usually associated with private homes. Because the trading room is the functional center of the business, the architects situated it between the partners' offices, and made it visible from the interior hallways. Here, 900 square feet of space, furnished with high-tech equipment, opens up into a trussed ceiling that liberates employees in their sense of community.

Facing page:
The original wood trusses impart an informal air to the trading room.

207

Above left:
The trading room encourages a sense of community.

Above right and facing page: The interiors promote a feeling of comfort usually associated with private homes.

209

Drawing left:
First floor plan,
entrance, reception,
conference room,
and offices

Drawing center:
Second floor plan,
trading room, and
typical offices

Drawing right:
Third floor plan,
offices

Pequot Capital Management, Inc.
Westport, Connecticut (1999)

Before renovation, this office included a large two-story space and a spiral staircase, as well as some glass-walled offices on the first floor. The company wanted to modify the overall appearance of the space, but maintain these features, along with the existing engineering systems. The CEO had already seen John Ciardullo Associates' ability to create a private/public continuum in the architects' design of the company's Southport office. He asked for a layout that would allow the corners to be semi-public common spaces, including an employee lounge and lunchroom. This setup situates the executive offices on the first floor, near the central trading room. Function, not superficial social status, was the criteria.

The CEO demanded the fulleast possible circulation and communication, and yet also a certain degree of privacy and quiet. In the second floor offices, the architects repeated the existing first floor pattern of offices, but used full-height glass partitions instead of half-height, thereby ensuring a reasonable degree of acoustic privacy while allowing constant visual communication. Glass partitions offer a clear view of the trading floor, while the partition support wall creates a comfortable, private seating area. To provide employees who work in interior first floor offices a view of the expansive lawns of the corporate park, the firm gave these offices glass partitions as well. On the second floor balcony, a half-height glass wall adds to the open atmosphere; employees are within an easy visual distance from the center of the firm's business.

Familiar with the CEO's love of basketball, John Ciardullo suggested in a lighthearted manner that the existing two-story space adjacent to the trading floor be turned into a half-sized court. The CEO agreed, and Pequot Capital Management became the kind of space where people could work, play, and enjoy genuine communication. The second-story interior offices have half-height glass partitions looking onto the court. Between the court and the trading room is an exercise area, separated from the court by a half wall, and from the trading room by a full wall.

To minimize traffic and distraction in the trading room, the architects directed circulation to the second floor with a stairway, which is cantilevered over the exercise room and bounded by the same half-height glass. At the top of the stairs, there are paths to the second-floor offices and the balcony that encircles the trading floor.

By realizing the possibilities inherent in the space and appropriate to the client, John Ciardullo Associates took this project to the level of "social work" in the best sense: working to encourage socializing and to kindle a sense of community.

Facing page:
The trading floor is clearly visible from the second floor offices.

211

212

213

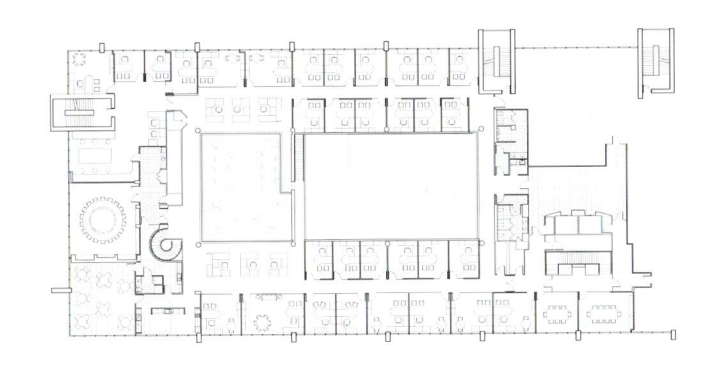

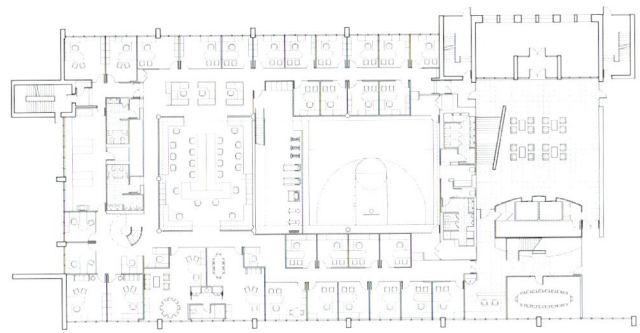

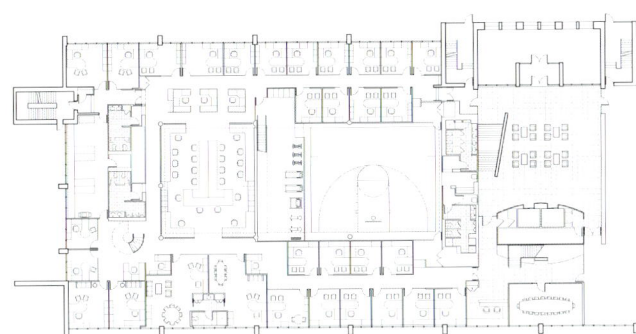

Facing page:
A half-sized basketball court gives employees a place to socialize and let off some steam.

Above:
Full-height glass partitions give both openness and privacy to the offices.

Drawing below:
First floor plan, trading room, basketball court, exercise room, and partners' offices

Drawing above:
Second floor plan, conference room, cafeteria, kitchen, and offices

Above left:
To minimize traffic in the trading room, circulation was directed to the second floor.

Above right:
The partners' offices look out onto the trading floor.

All above:
The partners' offices are outfitted with private bathrooms.

Pequot Capital Management, Inc.
New York, New York (2000)

For this highly visible space in the Citicorp Building in Manhattan, which complements the client's trading office in Westport, John Ciardullo Associates was asked to express the firm's stability and echo the social and cultural status of its clients without erring on the side of conservatism or formality. The architects used as much natural light as possible, optimized ceiling heights, and used a combination of metal and wood detailing to highlight or conceal various elements.

The site presented two distinct problems. First, each of the building's elevators services only even- or odd-numbered floors. The firm leases offices on the 34th and 35th floors, thus creating a circulation problem between these two 25,000-square-foot spaces. The second problem arose from the building's perfectly square floor plate. Original exposed diagonal steel bracing in the corners did not reflect Pequot's blend of flexibility and strength. In discussions with the client, the architects devised an overall visual theme of a circle in a square. This opposition is established by means of curves great and small, and materials that both soften the experience of moving through the large quadrangular space and symbolize the firm's credibility and strength: translucent glass, translucent acrylic, wood, and various forms of ornamental steel.

Visitors enter on the 35th floor and are immediately faced with a dramatic bridge, declaring the company's two floors and solving the circulation problem. The bridge conceals the office's mechanical systems. Its steel deck, finished with powdered epoxy resin, is bordered on one side by slightly curved translucent acrylic panels. Glass doors at the end of the bridge lead onto the slate-floored reception area, where the first shape to greet visitors is the curve of the reception desk, plated with 1/8-inch-thick steel.

Because this office space serves as a semi-public executive briefing center, the glass walls are symbolic as well as functional, providing only the slightest visual obstacle. Every straight line denoting a barrier is countered by a generous, open curve. Two rectangular conference rooms are visible from the formal reception space. Inside are opulent, distinctly textured tables, 12 feet and 20 feet in length, which were custom designed by the architects. These are crafted of sycamore with cherry trim and supported by cylindrical perforated steel legs. A trough running the central length of the tabletop, covered by a five-inch-wide steel plate and finished with a black matte stain, hides electrical boxes for electronic and voice data access. Raising the ceilings in the conference rooms and offices exposed overhead utilities and lighting fixtures. To conceal these, the architects suspended curved plates of 16-guage perforated steel. These curves soften the linear effect of the plate glass walls and windows opposite.

Great curving walls, implying a circle, center the 35th floor. On the 3rd Avenue side there is a curving wall of maple, which hides the mail and technical rooms. On the Lexington Avenue side, a wall of translucent glass panels and maple encloses a fitness room and a relaxation space furnished with lounge chairs and café tables and stools. In this way John Ciardullo Associates assured a semi-private space where employees can chat or work out, sharing a few leisure moments during the workday. To reinforce the luxury of the entire space, the client specified areas for art. On the exterior corners are the executive offices, furnished with round wooden tables that echo the great implied circle within the square.

Two steel staircases connect the 34th floor offices, each cantilevered from steel tube supports concealed within the adjacent wood-paneled wall. They are reinforced from below with a welded steel curved plate. All the office's steel is treated with the same black matte stain. This same elegant effect is achieved in the passage below the span of the pedestrian bridge, which is illuminated by fluorescent lights glowing through the irregularly curved, translucent acrylic panels.

**Facing page:
A convenient stair connects the 34th and 35th floors.**

217

In designing this opulent space, John Ciardullo Associates did not lose track of the ultimate goal, which is always to give the community at hand a sense of place. In this case, the community is made up of the executives and employees of Pequot Capital Management and their clients. Within the space, the architects provided some areas that are more public and some that are more private, clarified the circulation, and tailored every detail to the expectations of this community.

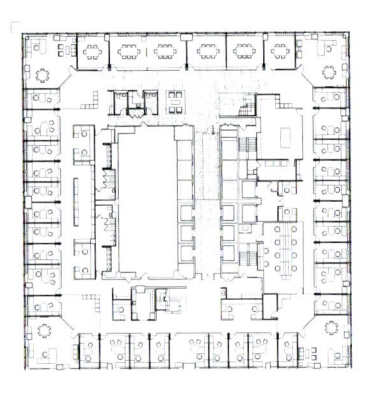

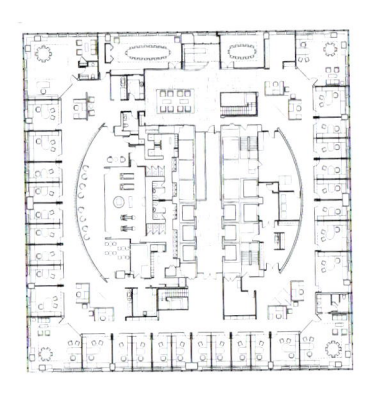

Drawings left to right:
34th and 35th floor plans.

Above:
Partner's office

Below:
Glass walls in offices and conference rooms create only the slightest visual obstacle.

Facing page:
A slate floor and curved steel desk greet visitors in the reception area.

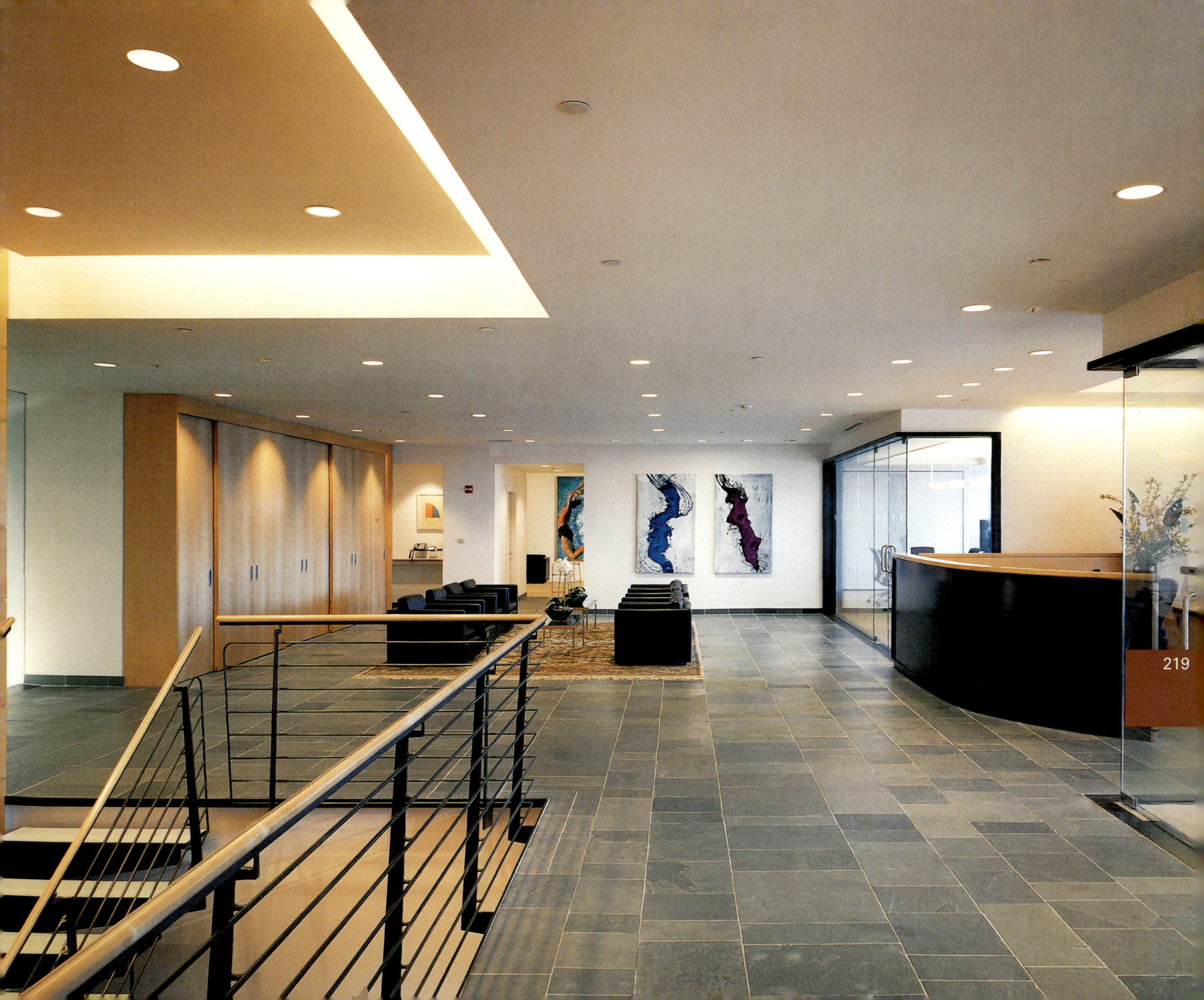

Left:
A curving wall of maple conceals the mailroom and toilets.

Middle:
Café tables outfit the recreation room.

Right:
On the 35th floor, every straight line indicating a barrier is countered by a generous, open curve.

221

All above:
Employees don't need to leave the office to travel between floors.

**Drawing above:
Section at
stair**

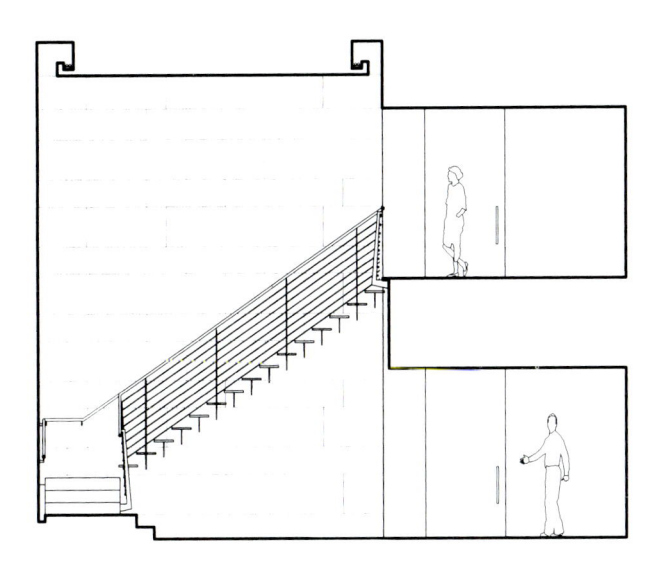

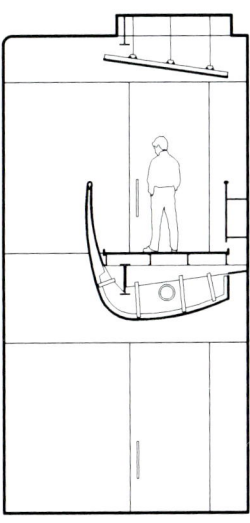

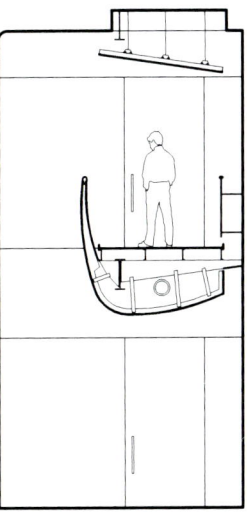

**Drawing below:
Section at entrance
bridge**

**All above:
Visitors enter on
the 35th floor
to a dramatic
steel and acrylic
bridge.**

223

224 Acknowledgements\Credits

Today, John Ciardullo Associates is known for community architecture, multi-family housing, planned communities, and schools. We've designed a good number of high-end private homes and corporate spaces as well, rounding out a nicely balanced body of work. Looking back, I can't help but fondly remember the beginning, when Paul Spears and I set up an office together. From the beginning we were like a team of explorers engaged in an all-consuming adventure. This monograph is an attempt to distill and describe our trek, in which each new commission has reiterated our conviction that architecture is a social occupation. My first and greatest thanks go to Paul.

My wife Mary has been integral to our growth and maturation. Her social sensitivity has served us and our clients since the beginning. Throughout this journey her presence and support have made the hard days easier and the rewards all the more enjoyable. I can't thank her enough.

This book depends upon the work it illustrates, and the work upon the dedication of the team of people we like to call "lifers and returnees." In addition to Paul and Mary, I thank Alyson Dunn, Charles Heaphy, Peter Kukresh, and Richard Piacentini. About ten years ago, John Ciardullo Associates evolved into a larger firm, since which time we've taken on bigger jobs, like public schools and the development of Rock Shelter Road. The core group of people who started working with us around that time has kept us a family. These members have grown with the firm, helping it grow in turn. To James Coley, Doug Currier, Stephen Kredell, Frank Lorino, and Stephen Rooney, my heartfelt thanks for the brilliant execution and management of many of the projects in this book. Elaine Pardalos stepped in at a vital moment, taking over all the work that isn't architecture and giving us the gift of time. My gratitude is hers. For encouraging us to elucidate the essential social facets of our architecture, I thank Anthony Iannacci and Edizioni Press. My thanks to Maggie for her understanding and insightful written interpretation of our thoughts. And because the only good architecture is living architecture, I thank the clients who have commissioned us to manifest social truths and expectations in architecture.

John Ciardullo

Boylan Street Pool
Newark, New Jersey (1975)
Project Team
Principal-In-Charge
John Ciardullo
Design Team
Paul Spears
Wayne Ehmann
Consultants
Structural Engineering
John Ciardullo Associates, P.C.
Mechanical Engineering
Marian Swiechowski
Site Engineering
John Ciardullo Associates, P.C.
General Contractor
Cedric Construction
Landscape
John Ciardullo Associates, P.C.
Client
City of Newark
Photography
Nathaniel Lieberman

St. Peter's
Park & Recreation Center
Newark, New Jersey (1976)
Project Team
Principal-In-Charge
John Ciardullo
Design Team
Paul Spears, Project Architect
Wayne Ehmann
Rocco Leonardis
Consultants
Structural Engineering
John Ciardullo Associates, P.C.
Mechanical Engineering
Marian Swiechowski
Site Engineering
John Ciardullo Associates, P.C.
General Contractor
Guasto Construction
Landscape
Miceli, Weed, Kulik
Client
City of Newark
Photography
Nathaniel Lieberman
Awards
-N.S.P.I. Gold Metal for Design Excellence in Public Pools
-International Awards Program 1978

South Paterson Public Library
Paterson, New Jersey (1978)
Project Team
Principal-In-Charge
John Ciardullo
Design Team
Paul Spear, Project Architect
Wayne Ehmann
Rocco Leonardis
Consultants
Structural Engineering
John Ciardullo Associates, P.C.
Mechanical Engineering
George Deng
Site Engineering
John Ciardullo Associates, P.C.
General Contractor
Franklin Universal Building
Landscape
John Ciardullo Associates, P.C.
Client
City of Paterson, New Jersey
Photography
Nathaniel Lieberman

Owen Dolen
Golden Age Center
Bronx, New York (1982)
Project Team
Principal-In-Charge
John Ciardullo
Design Team
Paul Spears, Project Architect
Richard Piacentini
David Nagrodsky
Gary Wells
Karen Settle
Consultants
Structural Engineering
John Ciardullo Associates, P.C.
Mechanical Engineering
George Deng
Site Engineering
John Ciardullo Associates, P.C.
General Contractor
Gabriel Construction
Landscape
John Ciardullo Associates, P.C.
Client
City of New York Department of Parks and Recreation
Photography
Nathaniel Lieberman
Awards
-1982 Award of Merit
-Cultural Structure
Best Application of Concrete in Design & Construction
The Concrete Industry Board, Inc. of New York

Isabelle Miller
Community Center
Camden, New Jersey (1982)
Project Team
Principal-In-Charge
John Ciardullo
Design Team
Paul Spears, Project Architect
Richard Piacentini, Project Manager
Wayne Ehmann
Karen Settle
Gary Wells
Consultants
Structural Engineers
John Ciardullo Associates, P.C.
Mechanical Engineering
Rubio Associates
Site Engineering
John Ciardullo Associates, P.C.
General Contractor
Fred Benson
Landscape
John Ciardullo Associates, P.C.
Client
City of Camden
Photography
Nathaniel Lieberman

Hamilton Fish
Park and Recreation Center
New York, New York (1992)
Project Team
Principal-In-Charge
John Ciardullo
Design Team
Paul Spears, Project Architect
Richard Piacentini
Peter Kukresh

Sandra McKee
Consultants
Structural Engineering
John Ciardullo Associates, P.C.
Mechanical Engineering
Rubio Associates
Site Engineering
John Ciardullo Associates, P.C.
General Contractor
AFC Enterprises, Inc.
Landscape
John Ciardullo Associates, P.C.
Client
City of New York Department of Parks and Recreation
Photography
Roy Wright
Awards
-The City Club of New York The 28th Bard Award for Excellence in Architecture & Urban Design 1995
-The American Institute of Architects New York Chapter 1994 Design Awards Program Architecture Awards Category
-American City & Country Ninth Annual Award of Merit 1992

Gerritsen Beach Branch Library
Brooklyn, New York (1997)
Project Team
Principal-In-Charge
John Ciardullo
Design Team
Alyson Dunn, Project Architect
Richard Piacentini
Peter Caradonna
Charles Heaphy
Consultants
Structural Engineering
John Ciardullo Associates, P.C.
Mechanical Engineering
Rubio Associates
Site Engineering
John Ciardullo Associates, P.C.
Landscape
John Ciardullo Associates, P.C.
Client
New York City Economic Development Corporation
Photography
Roy Wright

I.S. 254
Bronx, New York (1999)
Project Team
Principal-In-Charge
John Ciardullo
Design Team
Paul Spears, Project Architect
Frank Lorino, Project Manager
Jarrett Semkow
Consultants
Structural Engineering
John Ciardullo Associates, P.C.
Mechanical Engineering
Rubio Associates
Site Engineering
John Ciardullo Associates, P.C.
General Contractor
Canron/Innovax, LLC
Landscape
John Ciardullo Associates, P.C.
Owner
New York City Board of Education
Client
New York City School Construction Authority
Photography
Joseph Pisconeri Photography

P.S. 242
Queens, New York (2001)
Project Team
Principal-In-Charge
John Ciardullo
Design Team
Paul Spears, Project Architect
Frank Lorino, Project Manager
Jarrett Semkow
John Melton
Consultants
Structural Engineers
John Ciardullo Associates, P.C.
Mechanical Engineering
John A. Di Bari Consulting Engineers
Site Engineering
John Ciardullo Associates, P.C.
General Contractor
Citnalta Construction Corporation
Landscape
John Ciardullo Associates, P.C.
Design/Build Team
John Ciardullo Associates, P.C./ Citnalta Construction Corporation
Owner
New York City Board of Education
Client
New York City School Construction Authority

Edgemont Junior-Senior High School
Scarsdale, New York (2002)
Project Team
Principal-In-Charge
John Ciardullo
Design Team
Charles Heaphy, Project Architect
Naama Faucett
Natalie Kittner
Timo Lindman
Joan Malloy
Melaine Martin
John Melton
Priya Patel
Consultants
Structural Engineering
John Ciardullo Associates, P.C.
Mechanical Engineers
Clifford Dias P.E., P.C.
Site Engineering
John Ciardullo Associates, P.C.
Construction Manager
Andron Construction
Landscape
John Ciardullo Associates, P.C.
Client
Edgemont Union Free School District
Rendering
Kinetic Media, Inc.

**Seely Place
Elementary School
Scarsdale, New York (2002)**
Project Team
Principal-In-Charge
John Ciardullo
Design Team
*Charles Heaphy, Project Architect
Vini Babbar
Natalie Kittner
Timo Lindman
Joan Malloy*
Consultants
Structural Engineering
John Ciardullo Associates, P.C.
Mechanical Engineers
Clifford Dias P.E., P.C.
Site Engineering
John Ciardullo Associates, P.C.
Construction Manager
Andron Construction
Landscape
John Ciardullo Associates, P.C.
Client
Edgemont Union Free School District
Rendering
Kinetic Media, Inc.

**Greenville Elementary School
Scarsdale, New York (2002)**
Project Team
Principal-In-Charge
John Ciardullo
Design Team
*Charles Heaphy
Naama Faucett
Natalie Kittner*
*Melaine Martin
John Melton
Priya Patel
Bradley Watson
Mark Womble*
Consultants
Structural Engineering
John Ciardullo Associates, P.C.
Mechanical Engineers
Clifford Dias P.E., P.C.
Site Engineering
John Ciardullo Associates, P.C.
Construction Manager
Andron Construction
Landscape
John Ciardullo Associates, P.C.
Client
Edgemont Union Free School District
Rendering
Kinetic Media, Inc.

**P.S. 268
Queens, New York (2002)**
Project Team
Principal-In-Charge
John Ciardullo
Design Team
*Paul Spears
Charles Heaphy
Alyson Dunn
Frank Lorino
Doug Currier
Naama Faucett
Maria Idrovo
Natalie Kittner
Melanie Martin
Priya Patel*
Consultants
Structural Engineering
John Ciardullo Associates, P.C.
Mechanical Engineers
DVL Consulting Engineers, Inc.
Site Engineering
John Ciardullo Associates, P.C.
Landscape
John Ciardullo Associates, P.C.
Owner
New York City Board of Education
Client
New York City School Construction Authority
Rendering
Kinetic Media, Inc.

**P.S. 166
Queens, New York (2002)**
Project Team
Principal-In-Charge
John Ciardullo
Design Team
*Paul Spears, Project Architect
Peter Kukresh, Project Architect
John Fritz
Steve Rooney
Georgia Stokes*
Consultants
Structural Engineering
John Ciardullo Associates, P.C.
Mechanical Engineers
Rubio Associates.
Site Engineering
John Ciardullo Associates, P.C.
Landscape
John Ciardullo Associates, P.C
Owner
John Ciardullo Associates, P.C
Client
New York School Board of Education
Photography
Roy Wright

**Plaza Borinquen
Bronx, New York (1975)**
Project Team
Principal-In-Charge
John Ciardullo
Design Team
*Paul Spears, Project Architect
Wayne Ehmann
Rocco Leonardis
Gary Wells*
Consultants
Structural Engineering
John Ciardullo Associates, P.C.
Mechanical Engineers
Rubio Associates
Site Engineering
John Ciardullo Associates, P.C.
General Contractor
John Baranello and Sons, Inc.
Landscape
John Ciardullo Associates, P.C.
Client
South Bronx Community Housing Corporation
Photography
Nathaniel Lieberman
Awards
-City Club of New York Albert S. Bard Award for Merit in Civic Architecture

and Urban Design 1995
-New York Chapter
American Institute of Architects
1977 Residential Design Awards
Program

Maria Lopez Plaza
Bronx, New York (1982)
Project Team
Principal-In-Charge
John Ciardullo
Design Team
Paul Spears, Project Architect
Wayne Ehmann
Richard Piacentini
Consultants
Structural Engineering
John Ciardullo Associates, P.C.
Mechanical Engineers
Rubio Associates
Site Engineering
John Ciardullo Associates, P.C.
General Contractor
Marson Contracting Co., Inc.
Landscape
John Ciardullo Associates, P.C.
Client
South Bronx Community Housing Corporation
Photography
Nathaniel Lieberman

200 East 87th Street
New York, New York (1992)
Project Team
Principal-In-Charge
John Ciardullo
Design Team
Charles Heaphy, Project

Architect
Richard Piacentini
Peter Caradonna
Peter Kukresh
Jack O'keefe
Consultants
Structural Engineering
Andrew Gyimesi P.C.
Mechanical Engineers
I.M. Robbins P.C.
Site Engineering
John Ciardullo Associates, P.C.
General Contractor
Marson Contracting Co., Inc.
Landscape
John Ciardullo Associates, P.C.
Client
The Olnick Organization, Inc.
Photography
Roy Wright

Port Regalle
Staten Island, New York (1988)
Project Team
Principal-In-Charge
John Ciardullo
Design Team
Paul Spears, Project Architect
Sandra McKee, Project Manager
Richard Piacentini
David Nagrodsky
Peter Kukresh
Charles Heaphy
Gary Wells
Consultants
Structural Engineering
John Ciardullo Associates, P.C.
Mechanical Engineers

Rubio Associates
Site Engineering
Carmine Procassini
General Contractor
Port Regalle Partners, Ltd.
Landscape
John Ciardullo Associates, P.C.
Client
Port Regalle Partners, Ltd.
Photography
Nathaniel Lieberman
Awards
-Staten Island Chamber of Commerce Awards Excellence 1988
-Achievements, Nature Beauty, Craftsmanship, 26th Annual Chairman's Award,
Exterior & Interior Design

Rock Shelter Road
Waccabuc, New York (1998)
Project Team
Principal-In-Charge
John Ciardullo
Design Team:
Stephen Kredell, Project Manager
James Coley
Iris Katz
Consultants
Structural Engineering
John Ciardullo Associates, P.C.
Mechanical Engineers
John Ciardullo Associates, P.C.
Site Engineering
John Ciardullo Associates, P.C.
General Contractor
JTM Builders

Landscape
John Ciardullo Associates, P.C.
Client
John Todd Mead, Ltd.
Photography

Ciardullo House
Pleasantville, New York (1971)
Project Team
Principal-In-Charge
John Ciardullo
Design Team:
John Ciardullo
Consultants
Structural Engineering
John Ciardullo Associates, P.C.
Mechanical Engineers
John Ciardullo Associates, P.C.
Site Engineering
John Ciardullo Associates, P.C.
General Contractor
John Ciardullo
Client
John & Mary Ciardullo
Photography
Nathaniel Lieberman

Perless House
Greenwich, Connecticut (1982)
Project Team
Principal-In-Charge
John Ciardullo
Design Team
Paul Spears, Project Architect
Richard Piacentini
Karen Settle
Consultants
Structural Engineering

John Ciardullo Associates, P.C.
Mechanical Engineers
John Ciardullo Associates, P.C.
Site Engineering
John Ciardullo Associates, P.C.
General Contractor
Robert Perless
Landscape
John Ciardullo Associates, P.C.
Client
Mr. & Mrs. Robert Perless
Photography
Nathaniel Lieberman

Browne House
Waccabuc, New York (1990)
Project Team
Principal-In-Charge
John Ciardullo
Design Team
Paul Spears
Charles Heaphy
Sandra McKee
Peter Kukresh
Consultants
Structural Engineering
John Ciardullo Associates, P.C.
Mechanical Engineering
John Ciardullo Associates, P.C.
Site Engineering
John Ciardullo Associates, P.C.
Landscape
John Ciardullo Associates, P.C.
Client
Mr. & Mrs. Warren Browne
Photography
Nathaniel Lieberman

Torres House
Waccabuc, New York (1993)
Project Team
Principal-In-Charge
John Ciardullo
Design Team
Paul Spears
Charles Heaphy
Consultants
Structural Engineering
John Ciardullo Associates, P.C.
Mechanical Engineering
John Ciardullo Associates, P.C.
Site Engineering
John Ciardullo Associates, P.C.
General Contractor
John Ciardullo Associates, P.C.
Landscape
John Ciardullo Associates, P.C.
Client
Frank And Yolanda Torres
Photography
Nathaniel Lieberman

Samberg House
Chappaqua, New York (2001)
Project Team
Principal in Charge
John Ciardullo
Design Team
James Coley
Steve Kredell
Consultants
Structural engineers
John Ciardullo Associates, P.C.
Mechanical Engineers
John Ciardullo Associates, P.C.
Site Engineering
John Ciardullo Associates, P.C.
General Contractor
Luciano Valardo
Landscape
Melissa Bisbee Orme
Client
Arthur & Rebecca Samberg
Photo
Roy Wright

Dawson Giammalva, Capital Management, Inc., Southport, Connecticut (1997)
Project Team
Principal-In-Charge:
John Ciardullo
Design Team
Peter Kukresh
Consultants
Structural Engineering
John Ciardullo Associates, P.C.
General Contractor
Henry and Gerrety General Contractors
Client
Dawson Giammalva Capital Management, Inc.
Photography
Roy Wright

Pequot
Capital Management, Inc. Westport, Connecticut (1999)
Project Team
Principal-In-Charge
John Ciardullo
Design Team
Alyson Dunn
Consultants
Structural Engineering
John Ciardullo Associates, P.C.
Mechanical Engineers
Fletcher-Thompson, Inc.
General Contractor
Fusco Corporation
Client
Pequot Capital Management, Inc.
Photography
Roy Wright

Pequot
Capital Management, Inc. New York, New York (2000)
Project Team
Principal-In-Charge
John Ciardullo
Design Team
Alyson Dunn
Charles Heaphy
Consultants
Structural Engineering
John Ciardullo Associates, P.C.
Mechanical Engineers
Clifford Dias P.E., P.C.
General Contractor
S. DiGiacomo & Son, Inc.
Client
Pequot Capital Management, Inc.
Photography
Elliot Kaufman
Roy Wright